Théodore Hersart La Villemarqué

Ballads and songs of Brittany

Théodore Hersart La Villemarqué

Ballads and songs of Brittany

ISBN/EAN: 9783744785693

Printed in Europe, USA, Canada, Australia, Japan

Cover: Foto ©Thomas Meinert / pixelio.de

More available books at **www.hansebooks.com**

BALLADS AND SONGS OF BRITTANY

By TOM TAYLOR

TRANSLATED FROM THE "BARSAZ-BREIZ" OF VICOMTE HERSART DE LA VILLEMARQUÉ

WITH SOME OF THE ORIGINAL MELODIES HARMONIZED BY
MRS. TOM TAYLOR

WITH ILLUSTRATIONS BY J. TISSOT, J. E. MILLAIS, R.A., J. TENNIEL,
C. KEENE, E. CORBOULD, AND H. K. BROWNE

London and Cambridge
MACMILLAN AND CO.
1865.

INTRODUCTION.

THE Brittany which still retains so much of its ancient tongue, national character, and local usages, as to separate its population from that of the rest of France even more distinctly than the Welsh or the Highlanders are separated from the English, comprehends the three departments of Finistère, Morbihan, and the Côtes du Nord. These departments include the four ancient bishoprics of St. Pol de Leon, or the Leonnais, Cornouaille, Vannes, and Tréguier, each of which was formerly, and is still in great measure, a district with distinct dress, usages, and local character, both in the landscape and the people.

The Léonais (the Lemovicas of the Merovingian sovereigns) forms the extreme western horn of Brittany, and includes almost all the *arrondissements* of Morlaix and Brest. It is the richest and most varied region of Finistère. Its fields are fertile: its population (setting Brest aside as a French Portsmouth, only Breton in name), scattered in small villages or isolated farms, live a life of extreme simplicity, which still retains most of the characteristics of an age of faith. The church is the great point of reunion for the Léonards, its "*pardons*," or festivals of patron saints, furnish its great occasions of rejoicing; the "Day of the Dead"—the day after All Saints' Day—is its chief family commemoration. The whole population is in mourning: the day is spent in religious services, in masses and prayers for the dead. The remains of the supper, which crowns the offices of the day, is left on the table, that the dead may take their seats again round the remembered board. The festival of St. John—the Christian substitute for the Druidic Sun-feast—is still celebrated. Beal-fires blaze on every hillside, round which the peasants dance all night, in their holiday clothes, to the sound of the *biniou*—a kind of rustic hautboy—and the shepherd's horn, or of a rude music drawn out of reeds fixed across a copper basin. The girl who dances round nine St. John's fires before midnight is sure to marry within the year. In many parishes the curé himself goes in procession with banner and cross to light the sacred fire. A brand from it is preserved with reverence: placed between a branch of box blessed on Palm Sunday, and a piece of the Twelfth-night cake, it is supposed to preserve the cottage from evil by thunder. The flowers of the nosegay which crowns the beal-fire heap are powerful talismans against bodily ills. Intensity of religious faith, passing into the wildest, and often grossest superstition, is the dominant character of the inhabitant of the Léonais. He is grave, intense in his feelings, though reserved in the expression of them, distrustful of strangers, and profoundly attached to his own country, its beliefs and usages. His dialect is long-drawn and almost chaunt-like. His dress is dark, almost always black or dark blue, relieved among the men only by a red or blue scarf round the waist; among the women, by a white *coiffe*, like a nun's *béguine*. Marriages are contracted as readily and as improvidently as in Ireland: hospitality is a custom as well as a duty, and the poor, down to the most abject beggar, are "God's guests."

The Léonard presents the gravest side of the Breton character, and has more in common with the Welsh than with the Irish Celt.

But a parallel to the mingled joyousness and pathos of the Irish temperament is to be found in Brittany—among the Kernéwotes, the inhabitants of Cornouaille, the district which lies round the mountains of Arré, between Morlaix to the north, and Pontivy to the south, bounded by the Léonais northwards, and southwards by the district of Vannes. The northern portion of this region is wild and barren; the southern, in parts at least, smiling and amene. Its coast scenery, especially about Quimper, is grand and terrible. Round Penmarch (the Horse's head), one of the most westerly points of the Breton coast, the dash of the Atlantic on the rocky headland is as terrific as anything on our own Cornish coast. Under the shadow of this headland lay the town of Is, whose drowning is the subject of one of the ballads in this collection.

Till within the last forty years mass used to be served once a year from a boat on the Menhirien (or Druid stones), which at low spring-tides rose above the sea, and were believed to be the altars of the buried city, while all the fishing-boats of the bay brought a devout population of worshippers to this Christian sacrifice at Druid altars. The Kernéwote of the coast has many points of resemblance with the Léonard. Like him, he is grave almost to gloom, austere, and self-restrained. He dwells habitually on the sadder aspects of his faith, and celebrates most respectfully its sadder ceremonials. But the Kernéwote of the interior is the Irishman of Brittany, mingling with the pathetic ground-tone, which everywhere underlies the Celtic character, flashes of humour and joyousness, giving himself up with passionate impulsiveness to the merriment of the marriage-feast, the wild excesses of the carouse at the fair or opening of the threshing-floor, the mad round of the *jabadao*, or the fierce excitement of the foot-ball play or wrestling-match, which often winds up the Cornish *pardons*. His dress is of brilliant colours, always bordered with bright scarlet, blue, or violet: about Quimper are worn the *bargou-braz*, the loose, Turk-like breeches—a relic of the old Celtic garb. It is the costume of Cornouaille that is known popularly as Breton—the bright jacket and vest, often with the name of the tailor and the date of the make worked in coloured wools on the breast, the broad belt and buckle, the baggy breeches and gay leggings, and the hair falling on the shoulders from under a broad-brimmed felt hat, or on the coast, one with narrow brims, turned up at the edge, and decorated with a many-coloured woollen band, its ends flying in the wind. It is in Cornouaille that the old marriage ceremonial, with its elaborate diplomatic arrangements of *Bazvalan* and *Breutaër*,* is kept up with most state and lavishness of outlay. The wrestling-bouts of this region are the most sharply contested and numerously attended. It is remarkable that wrestling—essentially a Celtic exercise—is in England confined to that side of the island where the Celtic nationality retained its latest hold; and the wrestling practice of Cornouaille, even down to the favourite hugs and throws, may be paralleled by the laws of the game as still carried on

* See their songs in this volume, Part II.

in Cumberland and Westmoreland, or in Devonshire and our own Cornwall.

Tréguier, the third of the Breton districts having a distinct dialect and character, lies to the east of Léon, between it and Normandy, and includes the department of the Côtes du Nord. It takes in, besides the old bishopric of Tréguier, that of St. Brieuc, and part of that of Dol. The coast-line is less savage than that of Cornouaille, the air milder, the ground richer and better cultivated. It is emphatically the training-ground of the Breton priesthood, who receive their education in its seminaries, and who have so largely contributed to mould the Breton character and imagination, as well by their songs as by their religious ministrations. The character of the Trégorrois is less rugged and severe than that of the Léonard or the Kernéwote of the coast—less excitable than that of the Kernéwote of the mountain. There is something about it which, in comparison with the Breton character of other regions, may be called soft, gentle, and submissive. It is from its seminaries that the sentimental element infiltrates the popular poetry of Brittany. The Trégorrois is intensely religious, but attaches himself especially to those festivals of the Church which breathe hope and peace and goodwill. Nowhere in Brittany is Christmas observed so piously: nowhere are the places of pilgrimage so famous or so largely resorted to as the shrines of St. Mathurin or Montcontour, or of Our Lady of Succour at Guingamp. Tréguier is the fountain-head of the religious canticles which fill such a large space in the poetry of Brittany; and at Lannion are still played, or have been played within living memory, Breton tragedies like the old Celtic plays of our own Cornwall—historical as well as religious, lasting often for three days, and holding spell-bound, for many hours of each day, peasant-audiences assembled by thousands in the open-air theatre.

The Klöarek, or seminarist of Tréguier, is generally a young peasant of sixteen or eighteen, who, having shown some vocation for the Church or a turn for books, has been sent by his parents (exulting in the honour of giving a son to the priesthood) to one of the seminaries which stud the Côtes du Nord. His student-life is more like that of the Scottish peasant sent to Glasgow or Edinburgh, St. Andrews or Aberdeen, with the intention of becoming a probationer of the Kirk of Scotland, than anything in England, or than the sharply regulated existence of the ordinary seminarist of Italy or other parts of France. He lives not in a college, but in a garret—often shared with four or five companions of his own class. He ekes out the poor maintenance which his parents can afford him by hewing wood and drawing water, by serving about the inn-yards, and, if he is lucky enough to find pupils, by lessons in reading and writing at ten sous a month! His father or mother on market-day brings the weekly provaunt of the young clerk—a scanty pittance of black bread, butter, bacon, or potatoes.

The contrast between the rude misery of such a life and its destination to the awful and almost superhuman functions of the priest—the growing sense of culture and intellectual expansion warring with the hard facts of material existence—the separation from home pleasures and village intimates of both sexes —and the anticipation of a lot which isolates for ever from the delight of love and the happiness of family and fireside-life— are all provocative, according to the nature they work on, of sad and regretful emotion, or of a passionate and mystic asceticism. Both find natural expression in poetry; the regrets in elegy or idyllic song, the piety in canticles and hymns. It is, indeed, the Klöarek who is at once the hero and the poet of most of the Sônes, as the Breton songs of the former class are called; and the author of the Buhez or legends of saints, and *Kanaouen* or religious songs, dealing with such subjects as the farewells interchanged between soul and body at death, the horrors of hell, and the joys of heaven—the recital of which makes one of the principal entertainments of the *pardon*. Tréguier, thanks to its Klöarek, is the nursery alike of the elegiac and religious popular poetry of Brittany.

Vannes, which occupies the southern coast of Brittany, is the most thoroughly Celtic portion of the country. It is as thickly covered with cromlec'hs, lichvens, peulvans, menhirs, barrows, and dolmen,* as Léon is—or rather was before the Revolution—with Calvaries, bone-houses, wayside chapels, and shrines of the Virgin. On the heath of Lanvaux rises a forest of 120 *menhirs:* Trehorentec is a city of the dead, swelling with *barrows* innumerable: but all the Druidic monuments of Vannes, and of the world, not excepting Stonehenge, sink into secondary rank by the side of Carnac, with its eleven parallel ranges of *peulvans*, stretching for a length of more than two leagues to the horizon —huge blocks, many planted with the narrow end downwards, and some twenty feet in height.

Vannes, too, is the site of the most memorable scenes of Breton romance and mediæval history. Here is the castle of Clisson, the tower of Du Guesclin, the battle-field of the Thirty, the church of Ploermel with the tombs of the Dukes of Brittany,

---

* *Cromlec'hs* are Druidic circles; *lichvens*, two vertical stones with a third laid across; *menhirs* and *peulvans*, single stones set up on end; *barrows*, burial mounds; and *dolmen*, broad flat stones resting on smaller stone supports.

and the mystic forest of Broceliand, where Merlin lies in his enchanted sleep, under the spells of Vivien.

Vannes is the home of the legends of gnomes and spirits, of dwarfs and fairies that haunt rocks and woods, streams and fountains, of the *dus* and *mary-morgan*, the *poulpican*, and the *korrigan*.* The foot-ball play of the *Soule*, in which villages and parishes contend for the mastery, limbs being broken and lives often lost in the fierce excitement of the struggle, is now confined to the district of Vannes. It was this region which furnished the most desperate elements to the *Chouannerie;* and the historic ballads† recording the prowess of Beaumanoir and Tinténiac, Du Guesclin, Jannedik Flamm, and Pontcalec, or the still earlier heroism of Noménoë and Lez-Breiz, Bran and Alan-al-Louarn, are still the nightly entertainment of its tavern-parties, its family-feasts, and *pardons*.

Such are the leading divisions of the Breton population, among which has grown up, and is still preserved, a richer ballad literature, and a larger stock of popular idyllic and religious poetry, than exists in any part of Europe of the same extent. The national character and local circumstances of the Breton have singularly favoured the preservation and oral

---

* Celtic fairies of the woods, streams, rocks, and springs.
† See the following selection.

transmission of their popular poetry. They have always been a people set apart by blood, language, usages, and feelings, from the rest of France. The fusion of Celtic with the neighbouring nationality, which has effaced almost all traces of the race (except a few words of common use and names of places) in Cambria, Devon, and Cornwall, and has for centuries been actively at work even in Wales itself, has only begun to operate in Brittany since the Revolution, and at every step has been fiercely resisted. The upholding of national usages, faiths, ceremonies, traditions, and glories, has been ever a religion in Brittany; and for the mass of the people song has been the sole instrument of their preservation. Manners here still retain their antique stamp—often a rude one, but often also beautiful and pathetic. The poetry that wells out of the Celtic nature wherever it is left to itself, has not had its course checked or crossed in Brittany by such influences as the Protestant Methodism of Wales, or the war of religion and races in Ireland. Ballads and canticles that were sung in the tenth, twelfth, and fourteenth centuries, are still handed down, by recitation, from father to son, from mother to child, among the peasants, beggars, and wandering "crowders," who have taken the place of the old bards.

It is this essentially historical character which gives a distinctive peculiarity of the Breton ballads as compared with our own. Setting apart "Chevy Chace," the "Geste of Robin Hood"—if its songs can be called historical—and some of the Border ballads, our own ballad literature has no strictly historical character. It is so difficult to identify its personages and incidents with any particular period or place as, in nineteen cases out of twenty, not to repay the labour of the attempt. The Breton ballad, as a rule, is sharply and distinctly historical. There is hardly one of the collection in the "Barsaz-Breiz" the incidents of which cannot be referred to their date, place, and particular actors. As all true ballad literature is contemporary, it is a fair inference that these ballads were originally composed while the memory of their subjects was still recent, though, in the process of oral transmission for generations, they have of course undergone all manner of modification and mutilation. The Vicomte de la Villemarqué, the accomplished editor of the "Barsaz-Breiz" (or poetic treasury of Brittany), is a Breton, of old and noble family, inspired by that ardent love of his country and race which is the dominant feeling of the Breton. His mother—still I believe alive—many years ago began collecting the ballads and songs of the country, and he continued the work, aided not only by his own active researches, but by the clergy and resident nobles and gentry, without whose help—

beyond the range of his own family influence—he would have found it impossible to overcome the ingrained distrust of the Breton peasant. He informs us in his preface that his habit has been to obtain all the versions he could of the same ballad, and the only liberty he has taken has been in choosing between more and less complete versions—proceeding on the sound theory that the fullest in detail and most picturesque in colour were likely to be the oldest. The result has been a body of ballads with as distinct and consistent an impress of their time upon them as the very best preserved examples in the Border Minstrelsy.

Besides the literature of the *guerz*, or ballad, properly so called, whether it describe historical incident or individual adventure, of crime, sorrow, or suffering—for hardly one of the ballads is of a light or cheerful cast—M. de la Villemarqué has obtained from oral recitation portions of an older poetry, less popular, and the work of the comparatively cultivated and learned class of the later bards, whose epoch closes with the sixth century.

Of this order are the earlier examples in my selection—"The Wine of the Gauls," "The Prediction of Gwenc'hlan," "The Lord Nann and the Fairy," "The March of Arthur," "The Plague of Elliant," and "The Drowning of Kaer-Is."

Generally these earlier poems are distinguished by the presence of alliteration as well as rhyme, by the more or less complete division into triplets, and by a distinctly archaic impress in the manners described and the feelings of the singer.

After these come the historic and narrative ballads, which cover a time extending from the eleventh century to the present day. My present selection includes none subsequent to the later half of the fourteenth century. They bear few traces of modernisation, as far as I am able to judge. I cannot pretend to form any estimate of antiquity from the language, of which my knowledge—mainly derived from the study of the ballads themselves, with the help of M. de la Villemarqué's literal French translation, and Legonidec's Breton Grammar and Dictionary—is too imperfect to justify me in giving any opinion. But I can feel "the keeping" of the narrative, style, and thoughts, and I can detect scarcely anything by this class of tests that seems to me like modern interpolation.

Besides a selection from the historical ballads, which might have been doubled in bulk without introducing anything less vivid and stirring than is to be found in this volume, I have made a selection from the *sônes*, or idyllic songs of the peasantry, both those appropriate to peculiar occasions—as the "Songs of Marriage," of "The June Feast," "The Shepherd's

Call," "The New Threshing-Floor,"—and others, like "The Leper," and "The Miller's Wife of Pontaro," which approach more nearly to the ballad, and the second of which is an almost unique specimen of the satiric and humorous *guerz*, which form a large part of the stock of the travelling tailors or rag-gatherers (*pillaouer*), who, with the beggars and blind players on *rote* or *biniou*, are the chief minstrels of the Breton peasantry. There are also tender and pathetic occasional songs—such as "The May Flowers," "The Swallows," "The Poor Clerk"—which are generally due to the reveries and regrets of some young seminarist of Tréguier, but are sometimes also, as in the case of the two first mentioned, the composition of the peasants themselves.

My present limits have not allowed me to include examples of the religious canticles, which are as distinctive a feature of the Breton popular poetry as the historical *guerz* or the idyllic *sóne*. This want may be supplied, and my selection of historical ballads enlarged, should a second edition of this book be called for.

The conditions of space imposed on me, were there no other reason, would debar me from entering on a wider inquiry, which would not have been foreign to the nature of my work, and which has a deep interest of its own—a comparison of the popular poetry of Brittany with that of the other Celtic races in Ireland, Wales, and Scotland. But this would require a volume to itself, and I feel that the inquiry demands an amount of knowledge of the Celtic language and literature to which I make no pretensions. The subject is one well worth the attention of Celtic scholars.

All the Breton ballads are rhymed, the older ones being often alliterative as well. The commonest metres are a shorter iambic one of eight feet, in couplets or triplets (in the older examples), and a longer anapæstic one in quatrains. I can claim for my translations one merit, if they have no other—that is, the utmost fidelity to the originals, both in metrical form and in expression, that I could give it. The only liberty I have taken is an occasional resort to certain English ballad locutions and repetitions, which have their almost exact parallel in the Breton, and to a few Scotticisms, which, from the large proportion of Scotch and north-country ballads in our national stock of such compositions, have become almost a common property of the ballad style.

CONTENTS.

PART I.

HISTORICAL SONGS AND BALLADS.

	PAGE
THE WINE OF THE GAULS, AND THE DANCE OF THE SWORD	1
THE LORD NANN AND THE FAIRY	9
THE PREDICTION OF GWENC'HLAN	15
THE MARCH OF ARTHUR	23
ALAN-THE-FOX	27
THE DROWNING OF KAER-IS	31
THE EVIL TRIBUTE OF NOMÉNOË	39
BRAN	51
THE PLAGUE OF ELLIANT	61
THE RETURN FROM SAXON-LAND	67
THE CRUSADER'S WIFE	71
THE CLERK OF ROHAN	79
BARON JAUIOZ	93
THE GOSS-HAWK	103
THE FOSTER-BROTHER	109
THE NIGHTINGALE	119

	PAGE
"THE BATTLE OF THE THIRTY"	125
JEAN O' THE FLAME	135
DU GUESCLIN'S VASSAL	141
THE WEDDING-GIRDLE	149

PART II.

SONGS USED ON DOMESTIC AND FESTIVE OCCASIONS.

THE FLOWERS OF MAY	161
THE ASKING OF THE BRIDE	165
THE SONG OF THE JUNE FEAST	175
THE SONG OF THE NEW THRESHING-FLOOR	179
THE SHEPHERD'S CALL	183
THE LEPER	187
THE MILLER'S WIFE OF PONTARO	193
THE SILVER MIRRORS	197
THE CROSS BY THE WAY	201
THE SWALLOWS	205
THE POOR CLERK	209
THE SONG OF THE SOULS IN PAIN	213

APPENDIX.

ORIGINAL BRETON AIRS HARMONIZED	217

PART I.

HISTORICAL SONGS AND BALLADS.

THE WINE OF THE GAULS, AND THE DANCE OF THE SWORD.

(GWIN AR C'HALLAOUED, HA KOROL AR C'HLEZE.)

[THE "Gauls," whose wine is praised in this savage chaunt, were the Franks, on whose vineyards and cellars Gregory of Tours describes the comparatively uncivilised Bretons as making regular autumnal raids. Thierry, in his "Récits Merovingiens," supposes the chaunt here translated to be one of those in which successful forays of this kind were celebrated. It is still sung in the Breton taverns, but M. de la Villemarqué informs us that the sense of much of it is lost among the peasants from whose recitation he picked it up, and he is by no means sure either of the completeness of his own version, or of the correctness of his interpretation in all points. The wines of the district about Nantes seem to be referred to, as they are white. The other drinks enumerated—that made of mulberry juice, beer, mead, and cider—were in old times, and still are (the three latter at least), national beverages of Brittany. It is probable, as M. de la Villemarqué conjectures, that two chaunts are here welded together; the second, beginning at the thirteenth stanza, seems to be a fragment of the song that accompanied the old Celtic sword-dance in honour of the Sun. The language of this portion of the chaunt is more antique than that of the preceding stanzas. In both, however, the alliteration is nearly perfect—an acknowledged sign of antiquity. The rhythm suggests a measured accompaniment of tramping feet and clashing swords; and the wild chorus, invoking fire and sword, oak, and earth, and waves, carries us back to the early times of Druidic elemental worship, as the whole composition breathes a ferocious delight in blood and battle, smacking little of Christian doctrine or discipline.]

THE WINE OF THE GAULS,

ETTER juice of vine
　　Than berry wine:
　　Better juice of vine!
　　　　Fire! fire! steel, Oh! steel!
　　　　Fire, fire! steel and fire!
　　　　Oak! oak, earth, and waves!
　　　　Waves, oak, earth, and oak!

Better wine o' the year
　　Than our beer,—
Better wine o' the year!
　　　　　　Fire! fire, &c.

Better blood grapes bleed
　　Than our mead,—
Better blood grapes bleed!
　　　　　　Fire! fire, &c.

Better drink o' the vine
　　Than apple wine,—
Better drink o' the vine!
　　　　　　Fire! fire, &c.

Dunghill Gaul, to thee,
  Leaf and tree,—
Stock and leaf to thee!

          Fire! fire, &c.

Valiant Breton, thine
  The white wine,—
Valiant Breton, thine!

          Fire! fire, &c.

Wine and blood they run
  Blent in one,—
Wine and blood they run!

          Fire! fire, &c.

White wine and red blood,
  Fat and good,—
White wine and red blood!

          Fire! fire, &c.

Red blood and white wine,
  Bright of shine,—
Red blood and white wine!

          Fire! fire, &c.

'Tis the Gauls' blood
  Runs in flood,—
'Tis the Gauls' blood!
                    Fire! fire, &c.

I've drunk wine and gore
  In the war,—
I've drunk wine and gore!
                    Fire! fire, &c.

Wine and blood they feed,
  Fat indeed,—
Wine and blood they feed!
                    Fire! fire, &c.

II.

Blood, wine, and glee,
  Sun, to thee,—
Blood, wine, and glee!
                    Fire! fire, &c.

Glee of dance and song,
  And battle-throng,—
Battle, dance, and song!
          Fire! fire, &c.

Let the sword-blades swing
  In a ring,—
Let the sword-blades swing!
          Fire! fire, &c.

Song of the blue steel,
  Death to feel,—
Song of the blue steel!
          Fire! fire, &c.

Fight, whereof the sword
  Is the Lord,—
Fight of the fell sword!
          Fire! fire, &c.

Sword, thou mighty king
  Of battle's ring,—
Sword, thou mighty king!
          Fire! fire, &c.

THE WINE OF THE GAULS.

With the rainbow's light
  Be thou bright,—
With the rainbow's light!
    Fire! fire! steel, Oh! steel!
    Fire, fire! steel and fire!
    Oak! oak, earth, and waves!
    Waves, oak, earth, and oak!

THE LORD NANN AND THE FAIRY.

(AOTROU NANN HAG AR GORRIGAN.)

[The "Korrigan" of Breton superstition is found both in Scotland and in Ireland. "*Korr*" means dwarf, and "*gan*" or "*gwen*" is interpreted by M. de la Villemarqué "genius" or "spirit." The "Korrigan" is nearly identical with the "elf" of Scandinavian mythology, and Danish ballads may be found in which the "elf" plays exactly the same part to a belated hunter as the Korrigan to the Lord Nann in the following ballad. As in other cases, I have been careful to follow the metre and divisions into stanzas of the original. The latter is important, as the triplet always indicates considerable antiquity in Cambrian and Armorican rhymed compositions. The old Celtic bardism especially affected "triads," or division into threes.]

THE good Lord Nann and his fair bride,
Were young when wedlock's knot was tied—
Were young when death did them divide.

But yesterday that lady fair
Two babes as white as snow did bear;
A man-child and a girl they were.

" Now, say what is thy heart's desire,
For making me a man-child's sire?
'Tis thine, whate'er thou may'st require.—

"What food soe'er thee lists to take,
Meat of the woodcock from the lake,
Meat of the wild deer from the brake."

"Oh, the meat of the deer is dainty food!
To eat thereof would do me good,
But I grudge to send thee to the wood."

The Lord of Nann, when this he heard,
Hath gripp'd his oak spear with never a word;
His bonny black horse he hath leap'd upon,
And forth to the greenwood he hath gone.

By the skirts of the wood as he did go,
He was 'ware of a hind as white as snow;

Oh, fast she ran, and fast he rode,
That the earth it shook where his horse-hoofs trode.

Oh, fast he rode, and fast she ran,
That the sweat to drop from his brow began—

That the sweat on his horse's flanks stood white;
So he rode and rode till the fall o' the night.

When he came to a stream that fed a lawn,
Hard by the grot of a Corrigaun.

The grass grew thick by the streamlet's brink,
And he lighted down off his horse to drink.

The Corrigaun sat by the fountain fair,
A-combing her long and yellow hair.

A-combing her hair with a comb of gold,—
(Not poor, I trow, are those maidens cold).—

" Now who's the bold wight that dares come here
To trouble my fairy fountain clear?

" Either thou straight shalt wed with me,
Or pine for four long years and three;
Or dead in three days' space shalt be."

" I will not wed with thee, I ween,
For wedded man a year I've been;

" Nor yet for seven years will I pine,
Nor die in three days for spell of thine;

" For spell of thine I will not die,
But when it pleaseth God on high.

" But here, and now, I'd leave my life,
Ere take a Corrigaun to wife."

" Oh mother, mother! for love of me,
Now make my bed, and speedily,
For I am sick as a man may be.

" Oh, never the tale to my ladye tell;
Three days and ye'll hear my passing-bell;
The Corrigaun hath cast her spell."

Three days they pass'd, three days were sped,
To her mother-in-law the ladye said:

" Now tell me, madam, now tell me, pray,
Wherefore the death-bells toll to-day?

"Why chaunt the priests in the street below,
All clad in their vestments white as snow?"

"A strange poor man, who harbour'd here,
He died last night, my daughter dear."

"But tell me, madam, my lord, your son—
My husband—whither is he gone?"

"But to the town, my child, he's gone;
And at your side he'll be back anon."

"What gown for my churching were't best to wear,—
My gown of grain, or of watchet fair?"

"The fashion of late, my child, hath grown,
That women for churching black should don."

As through the churchyard porch she stept,
She saw the grave where her husband slept.

"Who of our blood is lately dead,
That our ground is new raked and spread?"

"The truth I may no more forbear,
My son—your own poor lord—lies there!"

She threw herself on her knees amain,
And from her knees ne'er rose again.

That night they laid her, dead and cold,
Beside her lord, beneath the mould;
When, lo!—a marvel to behold!—

Next morn from the grave two oak-trees fair,
Shot lusty boughs high up in air;

And in their boughs—oh, wondrous sight!—
Two happy doves, all snowy white—

That sang, as ever the morn did rise,
And then flew up—into the skies!

THE PREDICTION OF GWENC'HLAN.

(DIOUGAN GWENC'HLAN.)

[AMONG the bards who, in the fourth and fifth centuries of our epoch, resisted the invasion of Druidism by Christianity, the name of Kian, surnamed "Gwenc'hlan" (meaning "pure of race"), has been preserved to us in one of the fragments attributed to Taliesin, who speaks of him as one he had known in his youth, a composer of songs in honour of his country and its heroes. Nennius speaks of him, with Taliesin, Aneurin, and Llywarc'h Henn, as one of the most illustrious of bards "in poemate Britannico." Prophecies (*Diouganou*) ascribed to him existed in a MS. of the fifteenth century, preserved till the Revolution in the Abbey of Landévénec. This MS., in all probability the transcript of one much more ancient, perished in the Revolutionary troubles. Some fragments of it have escaped, which are quoted by M. de la Villemarqué, in which Gwenc'hlan appears in the triple character of wizard, instructor in agriculture, and warlike bard. It is to him in the latter category that the savage song here translated refers. It is known both in Northern and Lower Brittany, and exists in the dialect of Tréguier as well as in that of Cornouaille. It is in the form of a prophecy. The tradition is that Gwenc'hlan, being taken prisoner by a hostile prince, was by him blinded, imprisoned, and left to die in a dungeon. In this low estate Gwenc'hlan prophesies the defeat and destruction of the enemy. The poem has numerous points of resemblance with the surviving fragments of Taliesin and Llywarc'h Henn; and among them is the allusion to the three cycles of existence, a dogma of the Druidic faith. "I have been thrice born," says Taliesin.* "I have been dead: I have been alive: I am what I was. I have been a hind on the hill: I have been a gay-plumaged cock: I have been a dun fawn. Now I am Taliesin." Of course the language of this fierce denunciation has lost much of its antique character, but the grim savageness of its sentiment is as intense as ever.]

---

* "Myvyrian Anthology," vol. i., pp. 36, 37.

THE PREDICTION OF GWENC'HLAN.

HEN the sun sets and flood-tides roar,
I sit and sing beside my door.

When I was young I loved to sing;
Now I am old to song I cling.

I sing by night, I sing by day,
For all my heart within is wae.

If head be bowed, and heart be sore,
Reason enow have I therefor.

It is not that I go in fear,
I would not shake though death were near.

It is not fear of death; I trow
Of living I have had enow.

The hands that seek me not shall find,
The eyes that seek me shall be blind.

Little I reck what time may hide,
Man's weird is wrought in Fate's good tide.

The gate of death must thrice be past
By all, before they rest at last.

II.

I see the boar break from the wood,
His hurt foot leaves its print in blood.

Blood clots the jaws that gape for rage;
His bristles they show grey with age.

Round him a sounder of his brood,
All grunting, ravenous for food.

Lo, where a sea-horse braves the boar,
That all for terror shakes the shore!

He shineth white as shining snows;
Two silver horns his frontlet shows.

Beneath his feet white seethes the foam
With fires that from his nostrils come.

About him the sea-horses go
As thick as mere-side sedges grow.

"Hold firm! hold firm, horse of the sea!
At the boar's head! Strike lustily!

"The naked feet slip in the gore:
Strike swifter, sorer and more sore!

"I see the blood-gouts stream amain:
Strike harder yet, and yet again!

"I see the blood rise to the knee:
I see the blood spread like a sea!

"Strike harder! Strike at head and breast!
To-morrow thou may'st take thy rest.

"Strike hard! Strike, sea-horse, stout and strong!
Strike at the head! strike loud and long!"

III.

In my cold grave as I lay still,
I heard the midnight erne scream shrill.

He bade his eaglets to be yare,
And all the wild birds of the air.

Unto the wild birds he 'gan call,
" Up on your wide wings, great and small!

" No carrion feast of sheep or hound;
'Tis man's meat reeks up from the ground.

" Grey raven from the sea-cliff bare,
Tell me what quarry grip'st thou there?"

" There's a chieftain's head my claws between,
Wherefrom to pike the two red een.

" His two foul een they shall be mine,
For that his hand did tear out thine."

" Red fox, that wily art and ware,
Tell me what quarry grip'st thou there ?"

" I hold his heart in my jaw-bone,
That was as false as is my own.

" The heart that schemed to work thee woe,
Doomed thee to lingering death and slow."

" And thou, foul toad, what hast to do,
Squat by the corner of his mou' ?"

" I wait beside the traitor's lip,
To watch when forth his soul shall slip.

" In my foul form that soul shall dwell,
To quit him for his work of hell

" Wrought on the bard, that dwells no more
'Tween Roch-allaz and Porth-gwenn shore."

THE MARCH OF ARTHUR.

(BALE ARZUR.)

[M. DE LA VILLEMARQUÉ, to whom we owe the Breton original of "The March of Arthur," which he obtained from the recitation of an old mountaineer of Leuhan, called Mikel Ploc'h, informs us that these triplets were sung in chorus, as late as the Chouan war, by the Breton peasants, as they marched to battle against the Republican soldiers. The belief in the appearance of Arthur's host on the mountains, headed by their mystic chief,—who awakens from his charmed sleep in the Valley of Avalon whenever war impends over his beloved Cymry,—is common to all the Celtic races, and may be compared with a similar faith as to Holger among the Danes, Barbarossa among the Germans, and Marco among the Servians. Sir Walter Scott has recorded the belief entertained in the Highlands of the apparition of mounted warriors riding along the precipitous flanks of the mountains, where no living horse could keep his footing. The apparition of this ghostly troop is always held to portend war; and it is no doubt the same which the Celtic bard has here described as arrayed under Arthur. The ancient air to which the triplets are sung (which will be found among the musical accompaniments in the Appendix) is a wild and warlike march; and the peasant who chanted it to De la Villemarqué told him it was always sung three times over. The composition is an ancient one, and contains many words now obsolete in Brittany, though still found in the Cymric of Wales. The last triplet is a late addition.]

RAMP, tramp, tramp, tramp to battle din!
Tramp son, tramp sire, tramp kith and kin!
Tramp one, tramp all, have hearts within.

The chieftain's son his sire addrest,
As morn awoke the world from rest:
"Lo! warriors on yon mountain crest—

"Lo! warriors armed, their course that hold
On grey war-horses riding bold,
With nostrils snorting wide for cold!

"Rank closing up on rank I see,
Six by six, and three by three,
Spear-points by thousands glinting free.

"Now rank on rank, twos front they go,
Behind a flag which to and fro
Sways, as the winds of death do blow!

"Nine sling-casts' length from van to rear—
I know 'tis Arthur's hosts appear;—
There Arthur strides—that foremost peer!"

"If it be Arthur—Ho! what, ho!
Up spear! out arrow! Bend the bow!
Forth, after Arthur, on the foe!"

The chieftain's words were hardly spoke,
When forth the cry of battle broke—
From end to end the hills it woke :

" Be 't head for hand, and heart for eye,
Death-wound for scratch—a-low, on high,—
Matron for maid, and man for boy !

" Stone-horse for mare, for heifers steers,
War-chief for warrior, youth for years,
And fire for sweat, and blood for tears.

" And three for one—by strath and scaur,
By day, by night, till near and far
The streams run red with waves of war !

" If in the fight we fall, so best !
Bathed in our blood—a baptism blest—
With joyous hearts we'll take our rest.

" If we but fall where we have fought,
As Christian men and Bretons ought,
Such death is ne'er too early sought."

ALAN-THE-FOX.

(ALAN-AL-LOUARN.)

[ALAN, surnamed "of the Twisted-beard" in Breton history, and "the Fox" in Breton popular tradition, after a youth spent in hunting down the wolves and bears of our own island—according to the monastic chronicler of Saint Brieuc*—put himself at the head of the Bretons, in a determined and successful attack on the Normans, near Dol † (A.D. 937), and, after defeating them in a second engagement at Saint Brieuc, was hailed chief by the assembled Bretons. M. de la Villemarqué, after citing the historic references to the hero of this spirited ballad, states that he took it down from the recitation of an old peasant of Lan-huel-en-Arez, who in his youth had fought in the Chouan war, under Georges Cadoudal. M. de la Villemarqué asked him who was the chief referred to in the ballad: "General Georges, of course," was the reply. Cadoudal was, in fact, known among his peasant soldiers by the *sobriquet* of "the Fox," well earned by his sagacity and aptitude for stratagem. The Normans are here described as "Gauls" and "Saxons," the names generally given by the Bretons to all enemies of their nationality; and the allusion to "the short-haired ears" is explained by the Norman practice of cutting the hair and beard, in contradistinction to the fashion of the Bretons, who have always worn flowing hair and moustache.]

THE fox with a beard he yelps,—yelp yelp! yelp yelp! in the glades;
Strange coneys, to your burrows! His eyes are two bright blades!

* Quoted by Dom. Morice in his "Histoire de Bretagne."
† "Chronicon Nannetense," quoted by Dom. Morice, vol. i., p. 145.

His fangs are sharp; his feet are swift; his claws drop gore;
Alan-the-Fox he yelps—yelp yelp!—to war, to war!

I've seen the Bretons whetting their weapons, one and all,
Not on a Breton whetstone, but on harness of the Gaul.

I've seen the Bretons reaping upon the battle field,
'Twas not blunted sickles, but sharp swords that they did wield.

They reaped not our own buckwheat, nor the rye of our
  Bretayne,
But the beardless Saxon ears, and the short-haired Gaulish grain.

They are not flails of wood the Bretons take to thresh their wheat,
But stout staves shod with iron, and armèd horses' feet.

I heard the cry the threshers raise when they've threshed out
  all the corn:
It rang from Mount St. Michael to the valley of Elorn.

From the Abbey of St. Weltas to the point of Finisterre,
And to Brittany's four corners the Fox's fame did bear.

Honour and laud for ever be the Fox's due reword;
This song for aye remember, and give pity to the bard.

The bard who sung this song the first, song since hath never
 sung—
Ah me, the hapless singer! The Gauls cut out his tongue.

But if his tongue be severed, his heart e'en yet is strong,
And still his hand is stout on harp to shoot the shafts of song!

THE DROWNING OF KAER-IS.*

(LIVADEN GER-IS.)

[THE anonymous chronicler of Ravenna mentions a town, which he calls Kar-is, as existing in Armorica in the fifth century. Here ruled a prince called Gradlonvawre *i.e.* Gradlon the Great. Gradlon was the protector of Gwénolé, the founder of the first abbey established in Brittany. The following ballad (the original of which M. de Villemarqué obtained from the recitation of Thomas Pen-venn,— *i.e.* Whitehead—a peasant of Trégunk) narrates the popular tradition of the destruction of the town by the king's daughter, Dahut, who opened a sluice, which kept out the sea, by a key stolen from her sleeping father, after an orgie, at her lover's bidding. This tradition is common to all the Celtic races. It is found in Wales and in Ireland. In the former country the King is Seizenin, the drowned town Gwaelood, and its site in Cardigan Bay, where the fishermen still talk of the ruins of ancient buildings seen by them at the bottom of the sea when the tide is lower than usual. In Ireland the town is Neagh, and our readers will remember the allusion to the sunken town in Moore's graceful lines :

> " On Lough Neagh's banks when the fisherman strays,
> At the hour of eve's declining,
> He sees the round towers of other days
> Beneath the waters shining."

Gwezno, a Welsh bard, whose date is referred to the fifth century, but whose poems are found in a manuscript ascribed to the ninth, has a poem on the subject (included in the Myvyrian Archæology) which begins with the awakening of the king :

"Arise, oh Seisenin, and look forth—the land of warriors, the fields of Gwezno, are invaded by the sea ! "

---

* " Kaer-Is," *i.e.* Is-Town, "caer" being the same word that enters into our own *Car*-lisle, the Celtic " Caer-Leon,"—Caer-marthen—Caer-laverock.

A chronicler, whose work is preserved in the Chartulary of Landven, attributes to Gradlon the introduction of wine into Brittany.

Marie of France, who tells the story of the drowning of Is-town in one of her Lais (Gradlon-meur), speaks of Gradlon's horse as having saved his master's life for a long time by swimming, and as having become wild with grief when the king fell off at last, and was drowned.

In another version it is the princess who is drowned. Her father is bearing her off, en croupe, when an awful voice thrice bids him fling off the demon who sits behind him. He does so, and the inundation is arrested.

Before the Revolution, King Gradlon's statue, mounted on his faithful horse, used to stand between the towers of the Cathedral of Quimper, and every year, on Saint Cecily's day, a minstrel used to mount the croup of the royal charger, with a napkin, a flagon of wine, and a golden hanap, all provided at the cost of the cathedral chapter. He used to put the napkin round the neck of the statue, pour the wine from the flagon into the hanap, put it to the statue's lips, and then, draining the liquor, fling the hanap among the crowd gathered below, to do honour to the introducer of the grape.

The poem, says M. de la Villemarqué, from whose learned notes I have taken the above information, is very antique in rhythmical structure and in language.

Its rude picturesqueness needs no pointing out, nor the dramatic skill and life with which the action of the story is sketched out. In this respect these Breton ballads seem to me unequalled by anything of their class. As in all the other translations in this volume, I have been scrupulously literal.]

1.

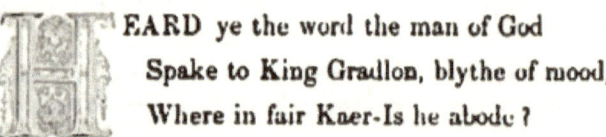EARD ye the word the man of God
Spake to King Gradlon, blythe of mood,
Where in fair Kaer-Is he abode?

"Sir King, of dalliance be not fain,
From evil loves thy heart refrain,
For hard on pleasure followeth pain.

THE DROWNING OF KAER-IS.

" Who feeds his fill on fish of sea
To feed the fishes doom'd is he ;
The swallower swallow'd up shall be.

" Who drinks of the wine and the barley-brew,
Of water shall drink as the fishes do ;—
Who knows not this shall learn 'tis true."

II.

Unto his guests King Gradlon said,
" My merry feres, the day is sped ;
I will betake me to my bed.

" Drink on, drink on, till morning light,
In feast and dalliance waste the night ;
For all that will the board is dight."

To Gradlon's daughter, bright of blee,
Her lover he whisper'd, tenderly :
" Bethink thee, sweet Dahut, the key !"

"Oh! I'll win the key from my father's side,
That bolts the sluice and bars the tide;
To work thy will is thy lady's pride."

III.

Whoso that ancient king had seen,
Asleep in his bed of the golden sheen,
Dumb-stricken all for awe had been—

To see him laid in his robe of grain,
His hair like snow, on his white hause-bane,*
And round his neck his golden chain.

Whoso had watch'd that night, I weet,
Had seen a maiden stilly fleet
In at the door, on naked feet,

To the old King's side, she hath stolen free,
And hath kneeled her down upon her knee,
And lightly hath ta'en both chain and key.

---

* "Hause," "hals bane," neck bone, often used in the old Scottish ballads.

IV.

He sleepeth still, he sleepeth sound,
When, hark, a cry from the lower ground—
"The sluice is oped, Kaer-Is is drown'd!

"Awake, Sir King, the gates unspar!
Rise up, and ride both fast and far!
The sea flows over bolt and bar!"

Now cursèd for ever mote she be,
That all for wine and harlotry,
The sluice unbarr'd that held the sea!

V.

"Say, woodman, that wonn'st in the forest green,
The wild horse of Gradlon hast thou seen,
As he pass'd the valley-walls between?"

"On Gradlon's horse I set not sight,
But I heard him go by in the dark of night,
Trip, trep,—trip, trep,—like a fire-flaught white!"

"Say, fisher, the mermaid hast thou seen,
Combing her hair by the sea-waves green—
Her hair like gold in the sunlight sheen?"

"I saw the white maiden of the sea,
And I heard her chaunt her melody,
And her song was sad as the wild waves be."

THE EVIL TRIBUTE OF NOMÉNOË.

(DROUK-KINNIG NEUMENOIOU.)

[NOMÉNOË was the Alfred of the Bretons, their deliverer from the Franks under Charles the Bald, in the 9th century (A.D. 841). He is a strictly historical personage. Under him the Bretons succeeded in driving the immensely superior force of the Franks beyond the rivers l'Oust and Vilaine; pushed their frontier as far as Poitou, and rescued from the hands of the invader the towns of Nantes and Rennes, which have remained included in Brittany from the date of their deliverance by Noménoë. This very spirited ballad was obtained by M. de la Villemarqué, from the oral recitation of a peasant of Kergerez. As in my other translations of Breton ballads, I have adhered to the metre and couplet divisions of the original, line for line.]

FYTTE I.

THE herb of gold* is cut: a cloud
   Across the sky hath spread its shroud.
      To war!

"The storm-wreaths gather, grim and grey,"
Quoth the great chief of Mount Aré.

"These three weeks past so thick they fall,
Towards the marches of the Gaul——

---

* The "herb of gold" is the mystic *seluye*. According to Breton superstition, iron cannot approach it without the sky clouding, and disaster following.

"So thick, that I no ways can see
My son returning unto me.

"Good merchant, farer to and fro,
Hast tidings of my son, Karò?"

"Mayhap, old chieftain of Aré;
But what his kind and calling say."

"He is a man of heart and brains,
To Roazon* he drove the wains;

"The wains to Roazon drove he,
Horsed with good horses, three by three,—

"That drew fair-shared among them all,
The Breton's tribute to the Gaul."

"If thy son's wains the tribute bore,
He will return to thee no more.

"When that the coin was brought to scale,
Three pounds were lacking to the tale.

* The Breton name of Rennes.

"Then outspake the Intendant straight:
'Vassal, thy head shall make the weight!'

"With that his sword forth he abrade,
And straight smote off the young man's head;

"And by the hair the head he swung,
And in the scale, for makeweight, flung."

The old chief at that cruel sound,
Him seem'd as he would fall in swound.

Stark on the rocks he grovell'd there—
His face hid with his hoary hair;

And, head on hand, made heavy moan:
"Karò, my son—my darling son!"

FYTTE II.

Then forth he fares, that aged man,
And after him his kith and clan;

The aged chieftain fareth straight
Unto Noménoë's castle-gate.

"Now, tell me, tell me, thou porter bold,
If that thy master be in hold?

"But, be he in, or be he out,
God guard from harm that chieftain stout."

Or ever he had pray'd his prayer,
Behold, Noménoë was there!

His quarry from the chase he bore,
His great hounds gambolling before:

In his right hand his bow unbent;
A wild-boar on his back uphent.

On his white hand, all fresh and red,
The blood dripp'd from the wild-boar's head.

"Fair fall you, honest mountain-clan,
Thee first, as chief, thou white-hair'd man.

" Your news, your news, come tell to me:
What would you of Noménoë ? "

" We come for right; to know, in brief,
Hath Heaven a God,—Bretayne a chief ? "

" Heaven *hath* a God, I trow, old man;
Bretayne a chief, if ought I can."

" He can that will, thereof no doubt,
And he that can the Frank drives out—

" Drives out the Frank, defends the land,
To avenge, and still avenge, doth stand ;—

" To avenge the living and the dead,
Me and my fair son foully sped ;

" My Karò, whose brave head did fall
By hand of the accursèd Gaul.

" They flung his head the weights to square ;
Like ripe wheat shone the golden hair."

Therewith the old man wept outright,
That tears ran down his beard so white,

Like dew-drops on a lily flower,
That glitter at the sun-rise hour.

When of those tears the chief was ware,
A stern and bloody oath he sware:

" I swear it, by this wild-boar's head,
And by the shaft that laid him dead,

" Till this plague's wash'd from out the land,
This blood I wash not off my hand!"

FYTTE III.

Noménoë hath done, I trow,
What never chieftain did till now;

Hath sought the sea-beach, sack in hand,
To gather pebbles from the strand—

Pebbles as tribute-toll to bring
The Intendant of the baldhead king.

Noménoë hath done, I trow,
What never chieftain did till now.

Prince as he is, hath ta'en his way,
The tribute-toll himself to pay.

———

" Fling wide the gates of Roazon,
That I may enter in, anon.

" Noménoë comes within your gate,
His wains all piled with silver freight."

" Light down, my lord, into the hall,
And leave your laden wains in stall.

" Leave your white horse to squire and groom,
And come to sup in the daïs-room :

" To sup, but first to wash, for lo!
E'en now the washing-horn * they blow."

" Fullsoon, fair sir, shall my washing be made,
When that the tribute hath been weigh'd."

The first sack from the wains they pight—
(I trow 'twas corded fair and tight)—

The first sack that they brought to scale,
'Twas found full weight and honest tale :

The second sack that they came to,
The weight therein was just and true ;

The third sack from the wains they pight—
"How, now! I trow this sack is light?"

The Intendant saw, and from his stand
Unto the sack he raught his hand—

---

* This practice of sounding the horn for washing before dinner (corner l'eau it is called in old French), is still kept up at the Temple.

He raught his hand the cords unto,
That so their knots he might undo.

" From off the sack thy hand refrain ;
My sword shall cut the knot in twain !"

The word had scantly pass'd his teeth,
When flash'd his bright sword from the sheath—

Through the Frank's neck the falchion went,
Sheer by his shoulders as he bent ;

It cleft the flesh and bones in twain,
And eke the links o' one balance-chain :

Into the scale the head plump'd straight,
And there, I trow, was honest weight !

Loud through the town the cry did go :
" Hands on the slayer ! Ho ! Harò !"

He gallops forth out through the night ;
" Ho ! torches, torches—on his flight !"

"Light up, light up! as best ye may,
The night is black, and frore the way.

"But ere ye catch me, sore I fear,
The shoes from off your feet you'll wear—

"The shoes of the gilded blue cordwain;*
For your scales—you'll ne'er need them again.

"Your scales of gold you will need no more,
To weigh the stones of the Breton shore!
        To war!"

---

* "Cordwain:" leather of Cordova—"Cordovan." Hence our "Cordwainer."

BRAN.

[A GREAT battle is recorded in history as having been fought in the tenth century near Kerloän, a village on the coast of Leon, between the Normans and the Bretons under Ewen the Great. The Normans were driven to their ships, but carried off some prisoners; among them the hero of this ballad, Bran, the grandson of a still greater chieftain of the same name, often mentioned in the Breton chronicles. Near Kerloän there is still a hamlet called after him, Kervran, or Bran's hold.

Many of the circumstances of the ballad—the disguise of the messenger, the tokens, the black and white sails (an incident as old as the Hellenic Theseus-legend)—are to be found in the *Romance of Tristan and Yseulde*, the author of which avows more than once his obligations to Breton popular song. M. de la Villemarqué calls attention to the use of the harp, here mentioned, as that instrument, still surviving in Wales, and till lately popular in Ireland and the Highlands of Scotland, has long been unknown in Brittany.]

SORE wounded lies the good knight Bran
On the foughten field of Kerloän.

On Kerloän field, hard by the shore,
Lieth the grandson of Bran-Vor.

Maugre our Bretons won the day,
He's bound and o'er sea borne away.

Borne over sea, shut up, alone,
In donjon-tower he made his moan.

"My kin they shout for joy, but I,
Sore wounded, on my bed must lie.

"Oh where shall I find a post to bear
A letter unto my mother dear?"

A post has been found, and in this wise ran
The orders of the good knight Bran—

"Now busk thee, busk thee in masquing weed,
A beggar's gown were safe at need.

"And take this signet ring o' me,
This ring of gold, for a token to be.

"To the land of Leon when thou shalt fare,
This ring to my lady mother bear.

"And if she come with my ransom-fee,
Hoist a white flag, that I may see.

"And if she come not, O dule and woe!
Hoist a black flag, that I may know."

II.

When the messenger came to the land of Leon,
The noble dame to supper had gone.

To supper was set, with her kinsmen all,—
The merry minstrels, they harp'd in hall.

" Fair fall thee, noble chatelan,
I bring this ring from thy fair son Bran.

" His ring of gold, and a letter thereon,—
Behoves you read it, and read anon."

" My merry minstrels, your harping give o'er,
With a heavy grief my heart is sore.

" No time for harping is this, God wot ;
My son lies bound, and I knew it not.

"To-night make me a good ship yare,
That to-morrow I over sea may fare."

III.

The morrow morn, from off his bed,
The good knight Bran to his warder said—

"Warder, warder, look out and see
Is there no ship upon the sea?"

"Now nay, Sir Knight, nought never see I,
But it be the great sea and the sky."

The good knight Bran, at mid of day,
Again to the warder he 'gan say—

"Warder, warder, look out and see,
Is there no ship upon the sea?"

"Now nay, Sir Knight, I see nought, I trow,
But the sea-mews flying to and fro."

The good knight Bran, at the set of day,
Again to the warder he 'gan say—

"Warder, warder, look out and see,
Is there no ship upon the sea?"

Outspake the warder, full of guile—
And smiled on him a cruel smile—

"A ship I see, far, far away,
And the winds about it lash the spray."

"What flag? what flag blows out to sight?—
Is't of the black? is't of the white?"

"Sir Knight, if rightly I discern,
'Tis black,—I swear by the brands that burn."

The woeful knight, when this he heard,
Thereafter never uttered word.

He turned his pale face to the wall,
And shivered as they that in fever fall.

IV.

The lady, as ever she leaped to land,
Bespoke the townsfolk upon the strand;

"What here has happ'd? what means this thing,
That thus I hear the church-bells ring?"

An aged man, that the ladye heard,
Made answer straight upon the word—

"One we had here in hold, a knight,
Is dead, so late as yesternight."

Scarce spoke were the words of that old man,
Distraught to the tower the ladye ran.

Oh! fast flowed her tears, as fast she flew,
With her thin white hairs all loose that blew,

That the townsfolk marvelled much to see
An aged ladye, of high degree,

A stranger ladye, in wail and woe,
And mourning, through their streets to go,

That each bespoke other, as by she ran,
" What ladye is this? what kith and clan?"

To the high tower foot when she won her way,
The porter the weeping dame 'gan pray.

" Draw bolt, draw bar, and let me in—
My son, my son! that to him I win!"

He hath drawn the bar, and the bolt hath sprung:
On her son's dead body herself she flung.

And in her arms she clasped him amain,
And from that embrace never rose again.

V.

On the battle-field of Kerloän,
There grows a tree looks o'er the lan';

There grows an oak in the place of stour,*
Where the Saxons fled from Ewen-Vor.

Upon this oak, when the moon shines bright,
The birds they gather from the night.

Sea-mews, pied black and white are there,
On every forehead a bloodspeck clear.

With them a corbie, ash-grey for eld,
And a young crow † aye at her side beheld.

Wayworn seem the twain, with wings that dreep,
As birds that flight o'er sea must keep.

So sweetly sing these birds, and clear,
The great sea stills its waves to hear,

And aye their songs one burden hold,
All save the young crow's and the corbie's old.

* "Battle"—frequent in our old ballads.
† "Bran," in all the Breton dialects, means a crow.

BRAN.

And this is ever the crow's sore cry,
"Sing, little birds, sing merrily.

"Sing, birds o' the land, in merry strain,
You died not far from your own Bretayne."

THE PLAGUE OF ELLIANT.

(BOSEN ELLIANT.)

[A LARGE proportion of the ballads still sung in the gatherings of the Breton peasantry—at the "pardon" of the patron saint, the festivities of the wedding, or the consecration of the new threshing-floor—relate to historical events of remote antiquity. One of these time-worn, but deeply-stamped pieces of old bardic coinage, now come down to exclusive circulation among hard peasant-hands, but still precious for the quality of its true poetic metal, and venerable for its ancient mint-mark, is the ballad of "The Plague of Elliant," of which the following is as literal a version, I think, as can be made from the Breton into the English. I have preserved the metre of the original, so that my version may be sung to the Breton air of the "Bosen Elliant." The plague which the ballad commemorates ravaged Brittany in the sixth century. The Book of Llandaff (in Jesus College, Oxford) contains an account of this plague, in an abridgment of the life of Saint Gwenolé, made in the ninth century by Gurdestin, abbot of the convent. In this account special mention is made of the ravages of the plague in the parish of Elliant, though the country immediately round about it is said to have been preserved from the scourge by the prayers of a saintly hermit named Rasian. He is mentioned in the ballad, which, like all other ballads in M. de la Villemarqué's *Barzas Breiz* (from which my translation was made), was taken down from oral recitation of the Breton peasantry.]

WIXT Faoüet and Llangolan
There lives a bard, a holy man—
His name is Father Rasian.

On Faoüet his hest he laid :
"Let every month a mass be said,
And bells be rung, and prayers be read."

In Elliant the plague is o'er,
But not till it had raged full sore :
It slew seven thousand and five score.

Death unto Elliant hath gone down,
No living soul is in the town—
No living soul but two alone.

A crone of sixty years is one,
The other is her only son.

"The Plague," quoth she, "is on our door-sill;
'Twill enter if it be God's will;
But till it enter bide we still."

Through Elliant's streets who wills to go,
Everywhere will find grass to mow—

Everywhere, save in two wheel-ruts bare,
Where the wheels of the dead-cart wont to fare.

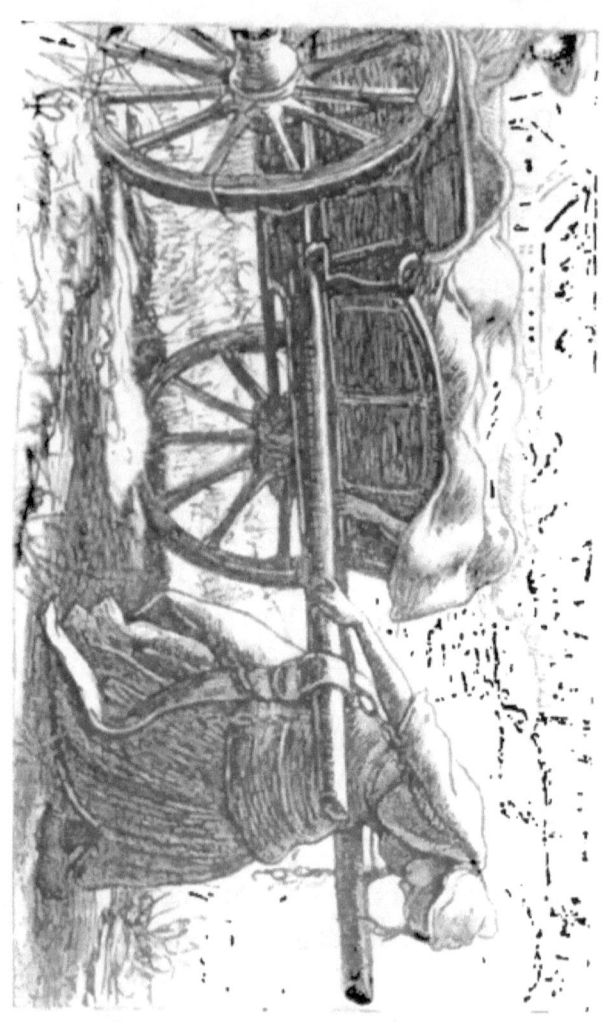

His heart were flint that had not wept,
Through Elliant's grass-grown streets who stept,

To see eighteen carts, each with its load—
Eighteen at the graveyard, eighteen on the road.

Nine children of one house there were
Whom one dead-cart to the grave did bear:
Their mother 'twixt the shafts did fare.

The father, whistling, walk'd behind,
With a careless step and a mazy mind.

The mother shriek'd and call'd on God,
Crush'd, soul and body, beneath her load.

"God, help me bury my children nine,
And I vow thee a cord of the wax so fine:

"A cord of the wax so long and fine,
To go thrice round the church and thrice round the shrine.

" Nine sons I had; I bare them all;
Now Death has ta'en them, great and small.

" Hath ta'en them all from my own door stone:
None left, e'en to give me to drink—not one!"

The churchyard to the walls brims o'er,
The church is full to the steps of the door:
They must bless fields, if they'd bury more.

There grows an oak by the churchyard wall,
From the top bough hangs a white grave pall—
The Plague hath taken one and all!

THE RETURN FROM SAXON-LAND.

(DISTRO EUZ A VRO-ZAOZ.)

[It is, at first blush, difficult to believe that a ballad of the date of the Conquest of England by William the Norman, and describing an episode in the life of one of the young Breton warriors who followed Brian and Alan, the two sons of Eudes of Brittany, to the muster of Duke William's array, should have survived to our own time. Yet such is the conclusion, not of M. de la Villemarqué only—who may be thought prejudiced by his strong national feelings as an Armorican—but of the grave historian Augustin Thierry, who, in his history of the Conquest, quotes this ballad as a contemporary composition. M. de la Villemarqué took it down from the mouth of Katel Road, a peasant woman of Nizon, in Cornouaille. The "wedding lace" referred to in the sixth quatrain was the emblematic tricoloured riband (white for innocence, rose-coloured for the beauty and hopes of the bride, black for the grief of her rejected lovers) which, in old times, it was the fashion for the *Diskared*—the chief of the discarded suitors—to fasten round the waist of the bride before she left her home for the altar. In return, he could claim a kiss. This riband was preserved, with the rest of the wedding paraphernalia, in the bride's chest, and was only brought out on occasions of high ceremonial. It was, says M. de la Villemarqué, as if by this act the rival tied the knot of wedded faith between his lost love and her husband, and it was the bride's duty to keep the riband till it was laid in her coffin. In the ballad a mother uses it, at once as a token of identity and a proof of the intensity of her maternal love, to tie about the neck of the carrier-pigeon her letter to her long-absent son.]

'TWIXT the parish Pouldergat and the parish Plouaré,
A menye of brave gentlemen are gathered in array,

Boune to march under the order of our Dutchess' her fair son;
From Brittany's four corners much folk to them has gone.

They are boune unto the war, over sea, in Saxon-land:
I have my son Silvèstik, whom they look for on the strand:
I have my son Silvèstik, and save him I have none,
And he is of the menye that with our knight has gone.

One night I could not sleep, as I lay my bed upon:
I heard the maids of Kerlaz a singing of my son:
Up in my bed I started, and made my heavy moan,
"Lord God! my son Silvèstik, where art thou now, my own?

"Perchance thou mayst be more than three hundred leagues
    away,
Or hast been flung in the great sea, unto the fish a prey:
Hadst thou stayed with thy father, hadst thou stayed, my son,
    with me,
In troth-plight fast ere this, it had been well with thee.

"Troth-plighted long ere this, and wedded thou hast been,
To Mannaïk of Pouldergat, the fairest on the green;

Thou hadst been here amongst us, with thy children at thy
    knee,
Waking the glad noise through the house that sounds where
    children be.

"A pretty pigeon, small and white, by my doorstead broodeth
    still,
In the hollow of the rock she broods, the rock that crowns the
    hill ;
A letter I will write, to her neck I'll tie it on,
With my wedding-lace I'll tie it, and he'll come back, my son.

"Now lift thee, pretty pigeon, on thy wings, for love of me,
And let them bear thee many a mile across the weltering sea ;
Let them bear thee many a mile over the salt sea foam,
To learn if my dear son yet lives, and bring me tidings home.

"Wilt thou fly unto the host, where they fight across the sea,
That thou mayst bring back tidings of my poor son to me ?"
"'Tis mother's pigeon, in the wood by our door that used to
    coo ;
I see its wings that sweep the waves the galley-mast unto."

THE RETURN FROM SAXON-LAND.

"I greet you fair, Silvèstik; this letter from your home
Your mother sends it to you, by me, across the foam."
"In three years and a day, fair bird, if so it may betide,
Say I'll be at my father's hearth and by my mother's side."

Two years passed slowly over; three years did waste and wane;
"Now fare thee well, Silvèstik, I shall ne'er see thee again!
Oh! if I found thy poor small bones tossed up upon the shore,
Oh! tenderly I'd gather them, and kiss them o'er and o'er."

The words were hardly spoken, when a galley of Bretayne,
Rent and riv'n from prow to tafrail, came driving o'er the main;
With never a helm to guide her, oars gone, and shattered mast,
Upon the rocks—a masterless and battered hull—was cast,

Full-freighted with dead bodies; none knows or e'er will know
How long that ship of death had been driving to and fro;
And there among the dead men, stiff and stark, Silvèstik lies,
But parent's hand nor sweetheart's in love had closed his eyes!

THE CRUSADER'S WIFE.

(GREG AR CHROAZOUR.)

[FAOUËT is a village about two leagues from Quimperlé, the Lords of which were a younger branch of the ancient Breton family of Goulenn. The Crusade here referred to, must have been the first of 1096, as the Breton Crusaders are described as wearing the red cross. In the later ones each nation bore the cross of its own colour, black being that of Brittany. The Breton Crusaders were really absent five years, and not seven.]

"UNTO our Lord his war I'm bound, the call brooks no delay—
Where shall I give my gentle dame in charge while I'm away?"
"Give her to me, fair brother-in-law, an if it please you well,
In bower, among my maidens, with seemly state to dwell.

"In bower, with fair attendance, among my maidens all,
Or, if it better please her, beside my dame in hall,
In the same vessels for them both my cooks shall dress the meat,
And at the self-same board with them she shall sit down to eat."

And soon a stately sight it was that youthful dame to see,
In the castle-court of Faoüet, among the gentilrie,
Each a red cross on his shoulder, with great horse and pennoncel,
To gather for the Holy War with the lord that loved her well.

He had not ridden many a mile beyond the castle wall,
When sullen speech and scornful that dame must brook in hall.
" Do off thy robe of grain, and don a peasant's gown of gray,
And up, and out to tend the sheep, lost on the heath they stray."

" Gramèrcy, gentle brother, what evil have I done ?
How shall I tend the sheep that in my life tent never none ?"
" If sheep thou never tended, 'tis time that thou begin,
Or with my lance right sharply I'll lesson thee therein."

For the space of seven long years she wept, a mournful thing,
At the end of seven long years she set herself to sing,
When a young knight, from the Holy War that homeward chanced to ride,
He heard a sweet voice singing upon the mountain side.

"Light down, light down, my little page, and hold my bridle-
    rein,
Up yonder, on the hill-side, I hear a silver strain,—
A little voice like silver upon the hill I hear,
The last time that I heard that voice was this day seven year.

"Good morning, pretty maiden, well have you dined to-day,
That here, upon the hill-side, you sing so glad and gay?"
"Oh! yes, fair sir, I well have dined, now thanks to God
    therefor,
All with a sweet dry crust of bread, out here upon the moor."

"Now tell me, pretty maiden, who guard'st the silly sheep,
If I may find a lodging in yonder castle keep?"
"Yes, of a sooth, good gentleman, within that castle hall
You'll find fair lodging for yourself, and for your steed a stall.

"And soft and warm the feather bed spread for your rest will
    be,
Such as I had in days gone by, when a husband cared for me.
'Twas not in fold, among the sheep, that then I slept for need;
I ate not then from out the trough wherein the dogs do feed."

" But tell me, tell me, pretty one, where now thy lord may be,
For methinks upon thy finger a wedding ring I see."
" Unto the Holy War, sweet sir, went this dear lord of mine,
Oh ! long and fair his golden hair hung down, as fair as thine."

" If long and fair hung down his hair, like mine, look well on
  me,
If I am not thy very lord, that went away from thee."
" Oh, yes! oh, yes! and I'm your love, your wedded wife am I,
The lady of Faoüet I was called in days gone by."

" Now leave thy sheep, my gentle love, upon the hills to stray,
And ride we to the manor; my wrath brooks no delay."
" Now welcome, gentle brother, now welcome frank and fair."
" How goes it with my lady, that I trusted to thy care ?"

" Sit, brother, sit ; brave rid'st thou back that brave didst ride
  away :
Thy lady, with the castle dames, hath ridden to Quimperlé,
To Quimperlé they rode this morn, for a wedding-feast is there ;
When they come back, thou'lt find thy dame all blithe and
  debonair."

"Thou liest in thy throat, foul thief; in beggar-maid's array
Thou sent'st her forth to tend the sheep, lest on the hill they
    stray.
By thy two eyes, thou liest, for thy lady she is here—
E'en now, behind the portal, her sobs are in thine ear!

"Hence, thy foul shame to bury! accursèd mote thou be!
Thy heart is full of evil, and steeped in feloniè.
Were not this house my father's house, wherein my mother
    died,
Thy blood were reeking on the blade that hangs against my
    side!"

THE CLERK OF ROHAN.

(KLOAREK ROHAN.)

[JEHANNE DE ROHAN, daughter of Alan, sixth vicomte, married, in 1236, Mathieu, Lord of Beauvais, son of René, Constable of Naples. She is the heroine of the following ballad; her husband's compound title being translated into its Breton equivalents—Traon (valley) and ioli (fair). Three years after the marriage, Duke Pierre Mauclerc took the cross, and was followed by many Breton Lords. There was a truce between the Saracens and the Lords of this crusade in 1241, when most of the knights re-embarked at Joppa. This corresponds with the duration given to the Lord's absence in the ballad. It is also proved by a record in the Ecclesiastical Records of Nantes, that Mathieu de Beauvais was summoned by the Bishop of Nantes in the same year to appear before the Archbishop of Bourges—

"Super inquisitione excessuum."

Whether these "excesses" were the murder of his clerk-cousin and his wife, as recorded in the ballad, is not known.]

FYTTE I.

IN the house of Rohan is a maiden fair,
   (No daughter besides her mother bare),
   Twelve years have passed o'er her gentle head,
   Ere she hath given her will to wed.

Ere she hath consented, as maidens use,
From knights and barons a mate to choose—
From barons and knights that made resort
To offer this lovely ladye court.

She looked at all, but her heart would stay
On none save only the Baron Mahé,
The lord of the castle of Traon-joli,
A powerful peer of Italie—
He only her heart could win and wear,
So loyal he was, and so debonair.

Three years, and half a year beside,
They passed in happy wedding-tide,
When came the tidings, near and far,
How Eastwards gathered the Holy War.

" As noblest of blood I first am boune
To take the Cross against Mahoune ;
So since no other choice may be,
Fair cousin, I trust my wife to thee.
I trust my wife, and my baby dear,
Good clerk, see no ill comes them near."

As morning broke—on his war-horse stout,
Armed at all points, he was riding out,
When lo, there came his ladye fair
Adown the steps of the castle-stair.

Her babe in her lily arms she bore,
And oh, but I ween her sobs were sore,
As anigh her husband's side she drew
And clung his armèd knee unto—
And as she clung, she wept amain
That the tears they flecked the steel like rain.

" My honey lord, for God's dear grace,
Leave not your wife in lonely case ! "
Her lord, sore moved, reached down his hand,
Where by his side she kept her stand.

And lovingly lifted her, louting low,
And set her down on his saddle-bow,
And there he held her a little space,
And gently he kissed her pale sweet face ;
" My Jannedik, darling, but dry thy tear,
Thou'lt see me again, before the year."

With that he took his little child
From off the lap of the ladye mild;
Between his arms the babe he took,
And he fixed on its face such a loving look—
"How say'st, my son? When tall and stout
With thy father will't ride to battle out?"

As he rode forth from his castle-hold,
There was weeping and wail from young and old;
From young and old came sob and cry,
But the clerk—he looked with a tearless eye.

FYTTE II.

The days they went, and the days they came,
When the felon clerk bespake his dame,
"The year hath drawn unto its close,
And so mote the war, I well suppose;
The war hath come to its end, perdỳ,
Yet comes not thy lord to his castle and thee.

"Now answer, sweet sister and ladye mine,
What whispers that little heart of thine?

Holds still the fashion for ladyes to stay
Sad widows, whose lords live far away?"

"Now peace, vile clerk—thy heart within
Is full, to running o'er, with sin—
Had he been here, who calls me wife,
'Twere pity of thee both limb and life."

When the clerk this heard, with an evil look
To the kennel his secret way he took,
And he hath ta'en his lord's best hound,
And his throat he hath severed, round and round.

He hath caught of the thick blood—hath caught of the thin,
And he hath written a letter therein;
Hath written and sent to the Lord Mahé,
Where far in the East he at leaguer lay.

And thus it ran, in the good hound's blood—
"Thy ladye, dear lord, is sad of mood.
Sweet ladye, she is sorry of cheer,
For an ill-hap late befallen here;

To the green-wood she went to hunt the roe,
And your good dun hound is dead, I trow."

The Lord Mahé read the letter through,
And this was the answer he sent thereto:
" Bid my sweet ladye smooth her brow—
Of the red red gold we have store enow.

" What if my dun hound dead should be ?
When I come I'll buy as good as he—
But say in the green-wood 'twere pity she ride,
For hunters are gamesome, and ill might betide."

FYTTE III.

A second time, to the gentle dame,
This felon clerk by stealth he came:
" Fair ladye, your beauty will fade away,
Thus weeping ever both night and day."

" Oh, little I reck of beauty and blee,
When my own true lord is away from me."
" If that your lord bide away from you,
'Tis that he's slain, or hath wed anew.

"In the land of the East there are ladies fair,
And eke with dowers both rich and rare—
In the land of the East are swords and strife,
And many a good knight leaves his life.

"Beshrew him, an if new wife he has wed;
Forget him, an if he be stricken dead."
"I'll die if he be wedded again:
I'll die if that he hath been slain."

"Who flings in the fire a casket of cost,
Because the key thereof is lost?
Far better, I ween, is a new new key,
Than ever the olden one mote be."

"Now avaunt, foul clerk, thine evil tongue
With lewdness and leasing is canker-clung."
The clerk he heard with an evil look,
To the stable his secret way he took.

There he was ware of his lord's destrier
The fairest steed in the country near—

As smooth as an egg, and as white as curd,
Fiery, and free of step as a bird;
That never meaner forage had seen
Than the crushed broom boughs, and the buckwheat green.

He hath aimed—he hath thrust, and his dagger hath gone
To the haft behind the broad breast-bone.
He hath caught of the thick blood—hath caught of the thin,
And he hath written this letter therein:

"An ill-hap hath befallen here—
Let not my lord make angry cheer—
From a merry night-feast as my dame rode back,
Hind leg and fore your best horse brake."

Oh, dark was the Baron's eye that read:
"Ill-hap, indeed! my destrier dead!
My dun hound gone, and my choicest steed!
Clerk-cousin—advise her to better heed!

"Bid her—but gently—not chiding her sore—
To such night-feasts that she go no more.

Not horses alone such junkets undo—
But marriages may be marred there, too."

FYTTE IV.

The days they went, the days they came,
When the felon-clerk bespoke the dame—
"Or give me my will, or ware my knife,
For I therewith will have thy life."

" A thousand deaths I'd rather win,
Than anger my God with mortal sin."
The clerk such answer he mote not brook,
So fierce a wrath his spirit shook.

His dagger forth the sheath he drew—
And he launched it at her straight and true—
But the ladye's white angel turned his hand,
And the dagger-point in the wall did stand.

And the ladye scatheless to flight hath ta'en,
And hath barred her door with bolt and chain—

But the clerk his knife from the wall plucked out,
As mad as a dog in the summer drought.

And down the castle stairs so wide,
Two steps to a bound, and three steps to a stride,
And to the nurse-chamber his way doth keep,
Where the babe was sleeping its quiet sleep.

The little babe lay all alone,
One arm outside the cradle thrown—
One little rosy arm outspread,
The other folded beneath its head.

The little heart all bare to the blow—
  *   *   *   *   *
Oh, mother, that weeping henceforth must go!

Again the clerk hath clomb the stair,
And in black and red hath written fair,
And fast and flyingly went his pen—
"Quick, quick, dear lord, ride home again.

"Ride home, as fast as fast may be,
Here's need that order were ta'en by thee.

Your hound is dead, and your white horse lost,
But 'tis not this that grieves me most.

" What's hound that's gone, or steed that's sped ?
Oh, and alas ! your babe is dead !

" The big sow hath eaten your baby bright,
The while my ladye was dancing light
With the miller—a gentle gallant is he—
In your garden he's planting a red rose-tree."

FYTTE V.

This letter it came to the Lord Mahé,
As home from the war he hath ta'en his way,
As his happy homeward way he hath ta'en
A march to the merry trumpets' strain.

The while he read the letter o'er,
His mood it kindled more and more,
Till when he had finish'd the clerkly scroll,
In his hands he crumpled the parchment roll.

And he tore it in pieces with his teeth,
And he trode it his horse's feet beneath—
" To Brittany—ho! fast—fast as ye may—
I'll drive my lance through him would delay."

Fast, fast, he rode to his castle yett
And struck three strokes on the oaken gate—
Three strokes he struck so loud and clear,
That all in the castle astert to hear.

The felon clerk, as the strokes he heard,
He ran to open with never a word—
" Clerk-cousin, accursèd mote thou be!
Did I not trust my wife to thee?"

In his open mouth he hath driven his spear,
That out at his neck the point came clear;
And hath sprung up the stair so fierce and fast,
And into his ladye's bower hath past—
And or e'er she spake word—that ladye true,—
With his sword he hath stabb'd her through and through.

FYTTE VI.

" Now tell me, Sir Priest, if told it may be,
What sight in the castle did ye see ?"
" I have seen a sight of woe, I ween,
That sadder ne'er in the world was seen—
A saint slain all for her love and truth,
And her slayer well nigh dead for ruth."

" Now tell me, Sir Priest, if told it may be,
What sight at the cross-roads did ye see ?"
" I saw a carrion corpse flung bare
To the beasts of the field and the birds of the air."

" And what did ye see in the churchyard green,
By the light of the moon and the starlight keen ?"
" I saw a fair ladye, in white yclad,
And she sat on a grave that was newly made.

" With a baby clasp'd her breast unto,
His little heart stabbed through and through ;
A dun deer-hound on her right did stand,
And a snow-white steed on the other hand.

"The throat of that hound it gaspeth wide,
There's a red red wound in that horse's side;
And they reach out their muzzles, lithe and light,
And they lick her hands so soft and white.

"And she strokes good hound and good horse the while,
And smiles on both with a tender smile;
And then the babe—as jealous he were—
He strokes the cheek of his mother fair.

"This sight I saw till set the moon,
And I saw but the mirk about and abo'on;
But I heard the clear sweet nightingale ring
The song that in Heaven the angels sing."

BARON JAUIOZ.

[LOUIS, Baron of Jauïos, in Languedoc, is an historical personage. He came to Brittany in the train of the Duc de Berry, his suzerain, when that nobleman with the famous Du Guesclin and the Dukes of Bourbon and Burgundy were sent thither by King Charles V. to drive out the English (1378). He fought also against the English bands in Flanders, and is recorded among the knights taking part in the leaguers and combats of Bornbourg, Ypres, Cassel, and Gravelines. He afterwards embarked for the Holy Land at Aigues-Mortes. His purchase and abduction of a young Breton maiden, who dies of grief, is traditional. M. de la Villemarqué obtained the ballad from the Breton lexicographer, Legonidec.]

AS I was washing, the stream hard by,
Sudden I heard the death-bird's * cry.

" Wot you, Tina, the story goes,
You are sold to the Lord of Jauïoz ?"

" Is't true, dear mother, the thing I'm told ?
Is't true that to Lord Jauïoz I'm sold ?"

* A little grey finch, with a plaintive note, common in the winter on the heaths of Brittany, so called by the peasants.

"My poor little darling, nought I know,—
　Go, ask your father if this be so."

"Father, dear father, say is it true
　That Lord Jauīoz I am sold unto?"

"My darling daughter, nought I know,
　Go, ask your brother if it be so."

"Lannick, my brother, oh, tell me, pray!
　Am I sold to that Lord the people say?"

"You are sold to that Lord the people say,
　You must up and ride without delay;

"You must up and ride to his castle straight,
　For your price has been paid by tale and weight:

"Fifty crowns of the silver white,
　And as many crowns of the gold so bright."

"Now tell me, tell me, mother dear,
　What clothes is't fitting I should wear?

"My gown of grain, or of grey, shall't be,
    That my sister Helen made for me?

"My gown of grain, or my gown of white,
    And my bodice of samite so jimp and tight?"

"Busk thee, busk thee, as likes thee best,
    Small matter, my child, how thou art drest.

"A bonny black horse is tied at the gate,
    And there till the fall o' the night he'll wait,—

"Till the fall o' the night that horse will stay,
    All fairly saddled to bear thee away."

II.

Short space had she rode when the bells of St. Anne,—
    Her own church bells—to ring began.

Then sore she wept, as she sat in selle:
    "Farewell, Oh sweet St. Anne, farewell!

" Farewell dear bells of my own countrie,
   Dear bells of the church I no more shall see!"

As on she rode by the lake of Pain,
   'Twas there she saw of ghosts a train,—

A train of ghosts all robed in white,
   That in tiny boats on the lake shone bright,—

A crowd of ghosts—that all for dread
   Her teeth they chatter'd in her head.

As on she rode through the valley of Blood,*
   The ghosts stream'd after like a flood;

Her heart it was so sad and sore,
   That she closed her eyes to see no more;

Her heart it was so full of woe,
   That she fell in swoon as she did so.

---

* The lake of Pain and the valley of Blood will recall to readers who know the ballad of Thomas the Rhymer, the weird scenery he traverses with the Queen of Faëry. In Celtic mythology they are stages on the road from this world to the next.

BARON JAUÍOZ.

III.

"Now, draw anigh, and take a seat,
　Until 'tis time to go to meat."

The Baron he sat in the ingle-place,
　And black as a raven was his face;

His beard and hair were white as snow;
　Like lighted brands his eyes did glow.

"I see—I see a maiden here,
　That I have sought this many a year.

"My bonny May, wilt come with me,
　One after one my treasures to see;

"From room to room to see my store,
　And count my gold and silver o'er?"

"Oh, better I'd bruik with my minnie to be,
　Counting faggots with her, than gold with thee."

"Come down to the cellar, ladye mine,
 To drink with me of the honey-sweet wine."

"Sooner I'd stoop to the croft-pool brink,
 Where my father's horses go to drink."

"Come with me from shop to shop, my fair,
 To buy a mantle of state so rare."

"Oh, better I'd bruik a sackcloth shift,
 An 'twere my mother's make and gift."

"Ye'll come with me to the wardrobe straight,
 For a trimming to trim your robe of state."

"Better I'd bruik the white lace plain,
 That my sister made me, my own Elaine."

"May mine—May mine—if your words be true,
 It's little love I shall have of you!

"I would that blister'd had been my tongue,
 Ere my fool's head ran on a leman young—

"Ere my fool's hand wasted the good red gold,
 For a maiden that will not be consoled."

IV.

"Dear little birds, I pray you fair,
 To hear my words, high up in air;

"You go to my village, and you are glad,
 I may not go, and I am sad.

"The friends that are in my own countrie,
 When you shall see them greet from me,—

"Oh! greet the good mother that me bare,
 And the sire that rear'd me with love and care,—

"Oh! greet from me my mother true:
 The old priest that baptised me too;—

"Oh, bid them all farewell from me,
 And give my brother my pardon free."

BARON JAUÏOZ.

V.

Two months or three had pass'd away,
    All warm abed the household lay,—

All warm abed, and sleeping light
    Upon the middle of the night.

No sound without, no sound within,
    When a gentle voice at the door came in:

"My father, my mother, for God's dear sake,
    Due prayer for me the priest gar make.

"And pray you, too, and mourning wear,
    For your daughter lies upon her bier."

THE GOSS-HAWK.

(AR FALC'HON.)

[This spirited ballad is the popular record of a peasants' war which broke out in Brittany A.D. 1008. Tradition ascribes the outburst to the oppression of the tax-gatherers charged to collect the taxes imposed by the Dowager Duchess Hedwig, wife of Duke Geoffrey the First. On his return from a pilgrimage to Rome the Duke was killed by a peasant woman, one of whose hens had been struck down by his falcon. She flung a stone at the offending bird, and brained the Duke by the same blow. This song is still sung in the Black Mountains of Cornouaille, where M. de la Ville-marqué picked it up from a wooden-shoe maker of Koatskirion.]

HE Count's hawk killed the gude wife's hen,
For quits the gude wife the Count hath slain,
For blood o' the Count, the land's in thrall,
Poor folk driven like beasts of stall,

Trod under foot by robber-bands,
Renders and reivers from Gaulish lands,
Renders and reivers, that pike and pull
At the call of our Dame, as cow calls bull.

Weary of waste, for bare need bold,
The young have risen, risen the old,
For the blood of a hawk and a hen, no mo,—
Bretayne is blood and fire and wo.

In the Black Hills, on the eve of St. John,
Met round the beal-fire thirty-and-one.
And Kado-Gann * i' the midst was he,
Leant on his fork of iron and tree.

"Say, porridge-eaters,† how shall it be?
Will ye buckle to tax and fee?
My mother's son, not a doit he'll pay,
'Bet' hang than starve,' is Kado's say."

"Never a sol will I pay, I swear;
My cattle are clemmed, my bairns go bare.
I swear the blazing brands upon;
So help me Saint Kado and Saint John!

"A broken man they have made o' me,
They've eaten me out of farm and fee:

---

* Kado the fighter. † "*Potred-iod*," eaters of boiled buckwheat.

Or ever I see the fall o' the year,
A beggar's bags I'll be fain to wear."

" With a beggar's bags you shall not go,
At my back you shall march, with many mo—
Of fighting and feud, if that's their will,
Or ere day dawn they shall have their fill!

" Ere dawn they shall have both feud and fight,
We swear by the sea and the lightning's light,
We swear by the stars and by the moon,
By the earth alow and the sky aboon."

Up he hath hent a blazing brand,
And every man took fire in hand,
" It's up and away, my merry men all,
Fast and first on Kerâran * fall."

His wife marched by him, the troop before,
And on her shoulder a graipe † she bore,

---

* The Breton name for Guerrande.
† " *Chrog*," a three-pointed digger for rooting up potatoes, &c., so called in the North.

And aye she sung, as she strode along—
"Up, lads, and out,—stout hearts and strong!

"It's not a beggar's bags to wear,
That twice fifteen man-bairns I bare:
It's not to carry the wood to ha',
Oh no, nor yet the stone to draw:

"Not to bear burdens like beasts of stall,
Did I, their mother, bear them all:
Nor yet to tread out the gorse, I weet,
The prickly gorse with their naked feet:

"Nor the lord's destriers to graithe and groom,
Nor to keep hounds fat and hawks in plume,
But the wrong to quit, and the right restore,
For this my thirty bairns I bore!"

From beal-fire unto beal-fire along,
The steep up-mountain paths they throng;
To the blare of sheep-horn and battle-cry,
And "to fire with the taxing varletry!"

When from the hills to the plain they bore,
They were three thousand and five-score;
But ere to Langoad they did bear,
They were nine thousand, counted fair.

And when they came to Keraran,
They were thirty thousand, every man,
Thirty thousand and fifteen-score,
When Kado bade "halt! we march no more."

He scarce had spoken the word well out,
When the gorse was piled, from the lands about,
Twelve-score loads round the wall there stood,
That the flames they leaped as they were wud.

A flame so fierce, a flame so fast,
That iron forks, as in forge, it brast;
And the bones of them that in it fell,
They cracked like the bones of the damned in hell.

And the taxing varlets they roared i' the night,
Like wolves in a pit-fall, for rage and fright,

And when the sun, i' the morn, did daw,
A heap of ashes was all he saw.

THE FOSTER-BROTHER.

(AR BREUR-MAGER.)

[THE legend of the love-tryst, made in life, but kept after death, by a ghostly lover on a spectral steed, who bears off the maiden behind him to the other world, is common to the old ballad literature of Germany, Denmark, Modern Greece, and Servia. Bürger's Leonora, a modernisation of the old German ballad, has given the story the widest literary circulation. But the most striking touches of the ghostly ride are to be found in the Danish *Aage et Else*, as in the Breton.

The relation of foster-brother- or sister-hood is a very binding one among all the branches of the Celtic race. It is still recognised as among the strongest of all ties in Ireland.

This ballad is interesting for its allusions to the Breton ceremonials of wedding and burial, including the sending round of the grave-digger with his bell to announce the news of death—in the words still used—"Pray for the soul that was . . . ." such a knight, gentleman, or labourer. The "lyke-wake," or watching and feasting by the dead the night before burial (though the word is Saxon, and the practice prevailed also among the Teutonic race, in our Island at least), is also eminently a Celtic usage.

The end of the ghostly ride, in the Breton—unlike that in Bürger's adaptation of the old German legend—is Heaven, not Hell. The lovers reach the Celtic Island of the Blest—that happy isle of Avalon—(the apple garden) where, conducted thither by the bards Taliesin and Merlin, in the green shadow of the fruit-laden trees, Arthur and his good knights repose and recover of their sore wounds got in the battle of Camlaun.

Procopius[*] records how the fishermen dwelling on the coast of Gaul, opposite Britain, at midnight hear at their doors a knocking without hands. On going down to the shore they find weird barques with no visible freights, but so heavily laden that

---

[*] *De Bello Gothico*, lib. iv. c. xx.

they can scarcely swim, their gunwales rising barely an inch above the water. These barques are laden with souls, whom it is the duty of these fishermen to row over to the opposite shore. An hour suffices for their passage with these freights of souls, though with their own boats a night is hardly enough for it.]

FYTTE I.

OF all the maids of gentle blood that are in this countrie,
 Was none so fair as Gwendoline, scant eighteen years had she:
Dead was the ancient lord her sire, mother, and sisters twain:
But for her step-mother, alack! the maiden went her lane.

'Twas pity still to see her weeping salt salt tears and sair,
On the threshold of the manor, she that was so douce and fair,
For her foster-brother's good ship looking ever o'er the foam,
Her only living comfort, longing sore for it to come;
For her foster-brother's good ship, looking wistful out to sea,
Six years had sped them slowly since he left his own countrie.

"Out of my sight and void the gate, go gather in the kine;
'Tis not to sit with folded hands I gar thee drink and dine:"

Two hours and three before the day she must rise up at her call,
In winter-tide to light the fire, and sweep both bower and hall.
And up and out for water to the Dwarf's Spring must she fare;
In mended crock must draw it, and in leaky pail must bear.

'Twas mirk mirk night and the water bright troubled and
    drumlie flowed
With the horse-hoofs of an armèd knight,—seemed that from
    Nantes he rode.
"Fair fall thee, gentle maiden: in troth-plight art thou tied?"
And she that sely was and young, "I know not, sir," replied.
"Art thou troth-plighted, maiden? I pray thee, answer plain."
"Now save thy grace, fair gentleman, no troth-plight have I
    ta'en."

"Then show thy step-mother this ring, and tell her, to a knight
Who came from Nantes-wards riding, that thou thy troth hast
    plight.
In Nantes a sore fight hath been fought—his young squire lieth
    low,
And deep and wide in the knight's own side a red sword-wound
    doth show.

"Natheless in three weeks and three days well cured that knight will be,
And will ride unto the manor, freck and fast, in quest o' thee."
Home fast she ran, and on her hand she looked at the ring o' gold:
It was her foster-brother's ring her finger held in hold.

FYTTE II.

One week had sped, two weeks had fled, two weeks and one beside,
And never to the manor-gate saw she that knight to ride.
Then up and spake her step-dame—"Daughter, behoves thee wed:
Counsel I've ta'en and found the man will best beseem thy bed."

"Saving your grace, good step-mother, husband me liketh nane,
But an it were my foster-brother, that hath come back again.
He hath given me his ring of gold, my wedding ring to be,
And freck and fast, ere the week is past, he'll come in quest of me."

"Peace, silly thing, with thy wedding ring! Speak me no
    speeches fine:
Or a hazel-wand I'll take in hand, to tame that tongue o' thine!
Will thee or nill thee, busk thee straight, for thy bride-bed
    prepare,
With Jobig Al-loàdek, my groom so young and fair!"

"With Jobig! Heaven forefend—so my bride-bed were my
    bier!
Mother, my own sweet mother—would God that thou wert
    here!"
"Out to the yard, my dainty dame, there weep and hang thy
    head;
Maugre thy puling and thy prayers, in three days look to wed!"

FYTTE III.

It is the ancient grave-digger, he goeth up and down,
Ringing his bell, to tell the tale of death, by tower and town.
"Pray for the soul, that was a knight, and did true knightly
    part,
While he was in the body, pure of soul and stout of heart.

"He hath been wounded deep and sore with a sword-stroke in
 the side,
Out over Nantes, of that sore stroke in foughten field he died.
To-morrow with the set of sun his lyke-wake will be dight,
And from the white church to the grave he'll be borne at
 morning light."

FYTTE IV.

"You are early from the wedding." "Early? Yes, and in good
 tide;
But the feast it is not over, nor the bedding of the bride.
I may not hold for very ruth, nor that sorry sight forget,
To see the lurdane neat-herd by that gentle maiden set.

"Around that hapless maiden, who wept for bitter woe,
No eye of all but tears let fall—the priest he wept also:
All wept that to the altar of our church this morning came—
Young eyes and old were weeping—all but that sore step-dame!

"The more the merry minstrels from the church-door played
 and sung,
The more they strove to cheer her, the more her heart was wrung.

They have set her on the daïs, at the top place of the board;
She nor bite of bread hath broken, nor drop of water poured.

"And when they had unlaced her, twixt the bride-bed sheets
    to lay,
She hath torn the bride-ring from her hand, her bride-lace
    flung away:
And she hath fled out in the night, wild with dishevelled hair;
She hath fled forth to hide herself, and ne'er a one knows
    where."

FYTTE V.

The lights were out: in bower and hall all slept, both old and
    young—
All save that rueful maid, that watched and wandered, fever-
    clung.
"Who's there?"   "'Tis I, my Nola;* thy foster-brother's here."
"'Tis thou, in sooth? Thy very self? 'Tis thou, my brother
    dear!"

    * Short for *Gwennola*—the Breton form of *Gwendoline*.

Forth she hath sprung, and closely clung on the croup of the
    white destrier,
Her little arm clasped round him, behind her brother dear.
"How fast we ride, good brother! five score good leagues and
    more!
How happy I feel near thee, as I never felt before!

"Is't still far off, thy mother's house? Fain, fain I would be
    there."
"Now clasp me close, sweet sister; we have not long to fare."
The howlets hooted and flew on before them as they rade;
The wild things of the forest from those horse-hoofs fled dis-
    mayed.

"Thy good steed gallops bravely, thine armour glinteth sheen;
I find thee taller than of old and fairer too, I ween:
Taller and fairer than of old: say, is thy manor near?"
"Now clasp me close, sweet sister; e'en now we shall be there."

"There is a chill about thy heart, a chill upon thy hand:
Thou'rt cold, my brother;—in thy hair I feel the death-damps
    stand."

"Now clasp me close, sweet sister: to my manor we are come,
Hear'st not the wedding minstrels that with music bid us home?"

The words were barely spoken, sudden the horse stopped still,
Shivered from crest to pastern, and neighed both loud and shrill.
It was a pleasant island, and all upon the strand,
Young men and gracious maidens danced, seemly, hand in hand.

Around them green trees grew about, set thick with apples red,
And behind, the sun up-rising lighted the mountain's head.
In the midst a streamlet sparkled along its thin bright track,
Whereof souls that had y-drunken straightway to life came back.

There was Gwendoline's good mother, there were her sisters twain,
And all was glee and gladness, cry of joy, and merry strain.

FYTTE VI.

From the white church to the grave-yard when the sun arose next morn
The maiden corse of Gwendoline by maiden-hands was borne.

THE NIGHTINGALE.

(ANN EOSTIK.)

[THIS ballad, or one on the same subject, was certainly popular before the middle of the thirteenth century, when Marie of France—the first Anglo-Norman poetess—translated it among her "Lais," giving it the name it still bears. She spins out the story to many times the length of the Breton, to the sad weakening of the dramatic power and simplicity of the ballad: but Marie has a sweetness of her own, with a love of nature, and a freshness of feeling, which recall our own Chaucer, who no doubt knew and loved her *Lais*. How much in his spirit is the following (I modernise the spelling) from her *Lai* of the nightingale :—

> "Longuement se sont entr'aimés,
> Tant que ce vint à un été,
> Que bois et près sont reverdis,
> Et les vergers furent fleuris,
> Et les oiselets par grande douceur
> Mènent leur joie ensum* les fleurs."

We may be proud to claim Marie of France—for all her addition—for our Anglo-Norman, not the French, Parnassus. She lived and wrote in the reign of Henry III., in England, probably among the Breton families planted in Yorkshire by Alan of Brittany, to whom William gave forty-two manors in that county, which afterwards formed the duchy of Richmond.]

THE young wife of Saint Malo hath gone
To her high bower window to make her moan.
"Out and alack! My heart is sore;
My nightingale will sing no more."

* "*Ensemble*," "Amongst."

"Tell me, young wife, that yestreen I wed,
Why rise ye so often from your bed?
So often, when sleeping you should be,
At the mid o' the night, from the side o' me?
With head uncoifed, and naked feet—
Thy reason for rising tell me, sweet."

"Dear husband, if I rise so light
Out of my bed, at mid o' the night,
'Tis that at my window it lists me so
To see the good ships pass to and fro."

"'Tis never for ship that sailed, I ween,
That so oft at your bower window ye're seen.
'Tis never for ship that swam the sea,
Nor yet for two, nor yet for three.
'Tis no more to see the ships go by,
Than the lady moon and the stars to spy.
Now rede me, rede me, my bonny bride,
Why every night ye leave my side?"

"I rise at the cradle side to peep,
To see my little son in 's sleep."

" A babe—a sleeping babe to see?
'Tis no more for that than for ship on sea.
Jape me no japes, no tales tell me!
Speak sooth, for sooth I will have o' thee."

" Now fume not, nor fret, my kind old man,
I'll tell thee truth, as truth I can.
I hear a nightingale every night;
In the garden he sings on a rose-tree white:
A nightingale every night I hear,
He sings so sweet, he sings so clear,
So clear, so sweet, so true doth trill,
Each night, each night, when the sea is still."

The old man when this tale he heard,
He thought the more that he spoke no word:
When the old man heard what the young wife said,
He vowed a vow in his old grey head—
" Or speak she false, or speak she true,
This nightingale I will undo."

To the garden, at morn, he his way hath ta'en,
And bespoken the gardener, fast and fain.

"Now lythe and listen, good gardenere,
There is a thing mislikes me here.
In my garden-close is a nightingale,
That for singing all night will not fail,
For singing all night, till dawn of day,
That I sleep no snatch, do what I may.
If ta'en to-night that nightingale be,
A good gold penny I'll pay to thee."

The gardener into the garden hath gone,
And a sely springe he hath set anon.
And a nightingale he hath caught therein,
And ta'en to his lord, his gold penny to win.
The lord, when in hand he held the bird,
With a cruel laughter his heart was stirred;
Its pretty neck he has wrenched and wrung,
And the bird in his wife's white apron flung.

"Hae here, hae here, young wife o' mine,
Thy nightingale that sang sae fine;
It is for thee I have had it ta'en:
Nae doubt, sweet May, ye'll to see it be fain."

Her bachelor, when this hap he heard,
He sighed and he spoke a heavy word:

" Now are we springed, my sweet and me,
No more each other o' nights we'll see,
No more speak lovingly and low,
As we wont, in the moonlight, at her window!"

"THE BATTLE OF THE THIRTY."

(STOURM ANN TREGONT.)

[THE following rough, but spirited Breton ballad—still sung at Breton festivals under its national name—is the popular account of one of the most gallant episodes of the intestine war between the rival houses of De Montfort and Blois, which ravaged Brittany from 1341 to 1364. There can be little doubt that it is contemporaneous with the incident it describes. Froissart has told the same story in one of the supplemental chapters of his Chronicle discovered by M. Buchon among the MSS. of the Prince de Soubise, and published by him in 1824. A *lai* by a northern *trouvère* on the same subject was discovered by M. de Fréminville, in the Bibliothèque du Roi, and printed by him in 1819, and again more correctly in 1827, by M. Crapelet.

This *lai* has been vigorously translated by Mr. Harrison Ainsworth,* with an introduction in which all the particulars of the combat, and its literary records, will be found.

In explanation of the grounds of this Battle of the Thirty, it should be stated that the cause of De Montfort was supported by the English under a leader called by the Chroniclers "Bennboure," "Bembrough," and "Brandebourg." The Breton equivalent *Pennbroch*, "Badger-head," points rather to "Pembroke" as the true version of the name. De Blois was the chief of the national Breton party. The thirty Breton champions in this combat were headed by Robert de Beaumanoir, the brother in arms of the Great Du Guesclin. His family adopted their motto, "*Beau-manoir, bois ton sang*," from the incident recorded in the ballad. De Beaumanoir had first challenged Pembroke to a single combat, or to a joust of two or three of his men-at-arms, against the like number of Bretons. Pembroke declined a single joust, as "a trial of fortune without result," but offered, with twenty or thirty of his fellowship, to meet the like number of De Beaumanoir's followers. Froissart describes the combat as one *à l'outrance* on foot, though the ballad-maker makes De Beaumanoir tell his men to "go at the horses with their bills." Horses, however, were

---

* "The Combat of the Thirty." Chapman and Hall, London. 1859.

used, in fact, at least by the Breton De Montauban, who is said to have decided the action in favour of his party by riding down the English in the mêlée, at a critical moment.

The scene of the combat was on a heath, near an oak tree, at a spot called *Mi voie*, as being "half-way" between the Castle of Ploermel, held by Pembroke and the English for De Blois, and that of Josselin, garrisoned by De Beaumanoir and his Bretons for De Montfort. The oak tree was felled in the wars of the League, and its place was long marked by a cross. This was thrown down at the Revolution, but the site has since been marked by an obelisk, with an inscription recording the combat.

The action was fought on the vigil of Mid-Lent, Sunday, corresponding to March 27th, 1351 (new style).

The ballad, of which I offer a literal, and all but line for line, translation, is in the metre of the original, was taken down, from the recitation of a peasant, by M. de la Villemarqué.]

I.—THE MARCH* WINDS AND THE SAXON FOEMEN.

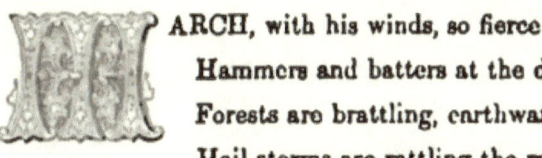ARCH, with his winds, so fierce and frore,
Hammers and batters at the door.
Forests are brattling, earthwards blown,
Hail-storms are rattling the roofs upon.

But not from hammers of March alone
Angry assault our roofs have known;
'Tis not alone the hail puts to proof
Toughness of rafter and stoutness of roof ;—

---

* The combat took place in March. One can imagine the contemporary bard seizing the idea of the inclement winds and rains of this stormy month as the best parallel to the violence and devastation of the English garrisons.

'Tis not alone the hail and the rain,
Beating the roof-tree, drowning the plain:—
Hail and rain, and winds that blow,
What are these to the Saxon foe?

II.—THE PRAYER OF THE THIRTY TO ST. KADO.*

" Blessed Saint Kado, that guard'st our land,
Strengthen us now in heart and hand ;
Grant that to-day, by aid from thee,
Brittany's foes may conquered be.

" If from the fight we e'er come back,
Golden baldric thou shalt not lack—
With sword and hauberk of gold thereto,
And mantle, to boot, of the welkin's blue.

" All shall say, when thine image they see,
Bless we Saint Kado on bended knee.
Up in high heaven, or here upon earth,
Where is the Saint that can mate him for worth?"

* St. Kado is our St. Chad.

III.—THE BATTLE OF THE THIRTY.

"Now count them, young squire, now count them for me,
And say what the tale of these knights may be."
"By one, two, and three I have counted them o'er—
There are knights fifteen, and as many more."

"If they are thirty, why so are we—
Upon them, gallants, right merrilié!
Let your bills on their horses be lustily laid:
No more shall they eat our buckwheat in blade."

Oh, heavy and hard were the blows that brast—
Not hammer on anvil falls more fast:
And fiercely and full ran the red, red blood,
As fierce and as full as a stream in flood.

And ragged and rent was their harness fair,
As the tattered rags of a beggar's wear;
And loud was the roar of the hot mêlée,
As the voice the great sea lifts alway.

IV.—THE PROWESS OF TINTÉNIAC.

Cried the Badger-head * to Tinténiac,
While he bore down fast as the driving rack,
"Try a thrust of my lance, Tinténiac—and see
If a truncheon of hollow reed it be."

"One thing, fair sir, shall be hollow anon,
And that is the head thy shoulders upon.
Where the corbies and crows will gather, fain
To pike and to pull at marrow and brain."

The words, I wis, were scarce spoke out,
Tinténiac hath swung his mace about,
And skull and helm and hood of mail
Hath smashed in one, as you'd smash a snail.

Keranrais laughed the blow to behold—
A laugh to make men's blood run cold—
"Were these stout Saxons all as thou,
Full soon they'd conquer our land, I trow!"

* "Pembroke," from the Breton *Penn*, head ; *brock*, badger.

"How many, sir squire, are left on the green?"
"The blood and the dust they blind my een."
"How many, sir squire, are left on the plain?"
"There are seven will never lift lance again."

V.—THE THIRST OF BEAUMANOIR.

Till the stroke of noon from the dawn of day
They fought, nor giving nor gaining way;
From the stroke of noon till the fall of night
Against the Saxons they held the fight.

"I'm athirst, sore athirst!" Lord Robert * he cried;
But Ar-Choad † flung back this word of pride
As you give back a sword-thrust sharp and sore—
"If thou'rt athirst, friend, drink thy gore."

When that sharp speech Lord Robert he heard,
He turned for shame, and he spake no word,
But he stormed like a fire on the Saxon foe,
And five stout knights on the sward laid low.

* De Beaumanoir.
† Ar-Choad means "of the wood" in the Breton. He is the Du Bois mentioned in the *lai*.

" Now count, sir squire, and tell to me,
How many Saxons yet left may be ?"
" My lord, I have told, and told them again,
By one, two, and three—but six remain."

" If six are left, they shall live their day,
But ransom, I trow, each man must pay—
A hundred pieces so bright and broad,
Wherewith to lighten the land's sore load."

VI.—THE RETURN TO CASTLE-JOSSELIN.

No true son of Bretayne were he
That in Josselin street had not crowed for glee,
As those good knights marched back from stour,
In every basnet a bright broom-flower—

Of the Breton no friend, I wis, were he,
Nor yet of the Saints of Brittanie,
Who had robbed Saint Kado of tribute due,
As patron of Breton knights so true—

Who had not rejoiced and his bonnet flung,
Who had not giv'n thanks, and this orison sung—
" Up in high heaven, or here, upon earth,
Lives not the Saint mates Saint Kado for worth !"

JEAN O' THE FLAME.

(JANNEDIK FLAMM.)

[THE heroine of this ballad (which M. de la Villemarqué took down from the recitation of a wandering blind beggar, Guillarm Arfoll, the same who sang to him the "Battle of the Thirty") is Jeanne of Flanders, the gallant wife of Jean de Montfort, the head of the Anglo-Norman (and at that moment also the Breton) party, whose struggle with the French faction under De Blois made Brittany the scene of incessant warfare for many years, about the middle of the fourteenth century. When Jean de Montfort, taken prisoner in Nantes, was carried off to Paris, his wife— "Qui bien," says Froissart, "avoit courage d'homme, et cœur de lion"—raised his fallen banner, and, like Maria Theresa in later times, presented herself, with her infant son in her arms, at Rennes, before the assembled barons, knights, and men-at-arms of the De Montfort following, and said to them: "Ha, seigneurs, be not discomforted nor dismayed for my lord whom we have lost. He was but one man. See here my little son, who shall restore him if it please God, and do you much good. I have means enow, whereof I will give freely, and promise you such a captain and guardian as shall mightily comfort you all." It was at the siege of Hennebont ("Qui était forte ville et grosse, et fort chastel"), into which she threw herself, that she fired the camp of Charles de Blois, as recorded in the ballad. This was in 1342. Froissart tells the story in his admirably vivid way in the 185th chapter of his "Chronicles."]

I.

"What is't that climbs the mountain's brow?"
"A flock of black wethers, as I trow."
"No flock of black wethers, nor yet of grey—
A menye of men-at-arms, I say—
Of men-at-arms from the land o' the Gaul,*
To lay a leaguer to Henbont Wall."

II.

As our Dutchess rode Henbont streets about,
Oh, leal and loud the bells rang out;
On her milk-white palfrey, bright o' blee,
Holding her babe upon her knee;
Nowhere she turned her bridle-rein,
But the Henbont folk shouted amain:
"God have mother and babe in grace,
And bring the Gaul to desperate case."

---

* As usual in the Breton ballads, the French are "Challaoued"—or "Vro-Chall"—Gauls; the English, "Saos," or Saxon.

The Dutchess had ridden so blithely by,
When from the Gauls there came a cry:
"Where lies the quarry the harbourers know,
We've slotted down both Fawn and Doe.
When Doe and Fawn alive we hold,
To bind them we've brought a chain of gold."

Down from the edge of the bartizan
Spake Jean o' the Flame, as 'twere a man:
"The Doe shall go safe and the Fawn fare free,
And the quarry a felon *Wolf** shall be!
Lest he shiver and shake for all his hair,
This very night we'll warm his lair."

Oh! an angry woman was Jean o' the Flame
As down the bartizan stair she came:
She hath donned a steel hauberk, breast and back,
And laced on her hair a basnet black;
She hath ta'en a sharp sword into her hand,
And hath chosen three hundred for a band;

---

* The Breton "*bleiz*," wolf, led to that animal being taken as the symbol of De *Blois* and his party.

And a red brand from the fire hath pight,
And out at a postern, through the night.

III.

The Gauls sang gay, the Gauls sang fine,
Set at the board drinking the wine.
In their pavilions close and tight,
The Gauls sang late into the night;
But their singing stinted, far and nigh,
When an eldritch voice was heard to cry:

"More than one mouth that laughs to-night,
Shall cry before the morning-light.

"More than one jaw that the white bread holds,
Shall take in its teeth the cold black moulds.

"More than one that red wine doth pour,
Shall soon be pouring out fat gore.

"More than one that boasts freck and free,
Ere morn a heap of ashes shall be."

There was many a Gaul that sat fordrunk,
With heavy head on the board y-sunk,
When through the tents an alarum past—
"The fire! the fire! To rescue fast!

"The fire! the fire! Fly one! fly all!
'Tis Jean o' the Flame, from Henbont Wall!"

Jean o' the Flame, I will go bound,
Is the wightest woman that e'er trod ground.
Was never a corner, far or near,
Of the Gaulish camp but the fire was there.
And the wind it broadened, the wind it blew,
Till it lit the black night through and through.
Where tents had been stood ash-heaps grey,
And roasted therein the Gauls they lay.
Burnt to ashes were thousands three,
Only a hundred 'scaped scot free!

IV.

Oh! a merry woman was Jean o' the Flame,
When at morn to her bower-window she came,

To see the plain all black and bare,
Grey ashes for pavilions fair;
And wreaths of smoke that curl and creep,
Up out of every small ash-heap.
Jean o' the Flame with a smile she sware,
"By God, was ne'er field burnt* so fair!

"Ne'er saw I field to such profit bren;
Where we had one ear we'll have ten!"

Still true the ancient saw is found,
"Nothing like Gauls' bones for the ground;
Gauls' bones, beat small as small may be,
To make the wheat grow lustilie."

* "*Pebes maradek*"—literally, "what a manuring by paring and burning."

DU GUESCLIN'S VASSAL.

(GWAZ AOTROU GWESKLEN.)

[BERTRAND DU GUESCLIN (1314—1380), Constable of France, born of an ancient Breton family, and one of the noblest preux chevaliers of whom the history of chivalry preserves record, is still a popular hero of Breton ballad and legend. This ballad tells the traditional tale of his razing of the Castle of Pestivien, one of the holds occupied by the English in the struggle of parties under De Blois and De Montfort.]

I.

IN the thick of Maël woods stands a stately castle-keep,
    With a turret at each corner, and a moat both wide
        and deep;
    In the great court is a well, where piled the bones of
        dead men lie,
And every night that bone-heap grows higher and more high.

On the windlass of that draw-well the corbies settle free,
And o'er their carrion-feast below—oh! but they croak merrilie.

That draw-bridge falleth lightly, but rises lightlier still;
Whoso lists therein may enter, but goes not out who will.

II.

A young squire through the Saxon pale on *chevauchie** did fare,
Iann Pontorson he was hight, a gentle squire and fair:
And as he rode at evenfall this stately castle by,
He asked of the chief warder leave therein that night to lie.

"Light down, light down, Sir Squire; for thee I'll let the draw-
    bridge fall.
Now lead thy red-roan courser in, and stable him in stall;
There he shall eat his fill o' the hay and of the barley fine,
Whilst you in hall, with our merry men all, shall sit you down
    to dine."

He is set at board, but never a word spake any there, I ween;
Nor knight, nor squire, nor man-at-arms—dumb men they might
    have been—

---

* No reader of Froissart can have forgotten the *chevauchies* or ridings out in quest of gallant adventures of arms, which give such an individual life and interest to his "Chronicles."

But 'twere a word to the maiden: "Biganna, mount the stair,
And see that for this stranger squire the bed be dighted yare."

When meat was done and boards were drawn, and the time for
    bed was come,
The gentle squire he clomb the stair into an upper room;
And blithe sang Iann Pontorson for his bed as he was boune,
And he set his horn of ivory on the bed-stock adown.

"Biganna, pretty sister, now say what this may be,
That ever ye sigh so heavilie as ye turn your looks on me?"
"Oh! if ye stood but where I stand, and knew the thing I
    know,
It's you would sigh, as you look'd on me, as heavily, I trow.—

"It's you would sigh as heavily, for very ruth, I ween:
Under the pillow at your bed-head there's a dagger bright and
    keen.
On blade and haft there's blood still left, that's not had time to
    dry:
'Tis the third man's blood that it has shed, and you must be
    fourth to die.

"Your gold and eke your white monie, your arms, and all your
    gear,
But an it be your red-roan horse, are ta'en and lock-fast here."
Under the pillow at his bed-head lightly his hand he laid,
And hath found the dagger with the blood still wet on haft and
    blade.

"Biganna, my sweet sister, now help me to win free,
And thou shalt have five hundred crowns all for a ransom-fee."
"Gramercy, sir; an asking I would ask, and only one:
It is—have you a wedded wife at home, or have you none?"

"False answer to thy asking will I none, betide what may;
A wedded wife I've had at home this two weeks and a day.
But I have three brothers, every one a better man than me:
For pleasure of thy heart choose one of them thy groom to be."

"For my heart there is no pleasure in man's love nor yet in fee;
There is no pleasure for my heart, but only, sir, in thee.
Follow me out, and never doubt but the draw-bridge we shall
    clear:
The porter will not stay us; he's my foster-brother dear."

Featly and fast the gate they've past, out o'er the bridge
    they've gone.
"Now up and ride, sweet sister, on the croup of my red roan.
The way lies free to Gwengamp: to my good Lord I'll go,
To ask if he hold dearly by his vassal's life or no:
Now ride we straight to Gwengamp, to my true Lord Gweaklèn,
That he come and lay a leaguer about Pestivien."

III.

"Fair greeting, men of Gwengamp, all for your courtesie,
I seek my good Lord Gweaklen; I pray you, where is he?"
"If you seek the good Lord Gweaklen, as so I read your
    call,
In the square-tower you'll find him, set in the Barons' Hall."

Oh! lightly Ian Pontorson within the hall has stept,
And straight to the Lord Gwesklen his forward way hath
    kept:
"The grace of God be with my Lord, and shield him from all
    harm,
Even as to shield his vassals my Lord holds out his arm."

"The grace of God be with thee, that speak'st so courteouslie,
He whom God shields to others at need a shield should be.
What need is thine? Short speech and sooth is that which
    likes me best."
"Needs one to harry Pestien—that bloody robbers' nest.

"'Tis thence the Saxon reivers on foray sally out,
Is never herd nor homestead safe for seven good leagues
    about:
And whoso enters Pestien Gate an ill death he must dree;
But an it were this maiden, they had made an end o' me.

"I trow they had slit my weasand, as they've slit many a score,"
And he up and out with the dagger that still was red with
    gore.
Then outspake Gwesklen: "By the saints that Bretons have in
    awe,
So long as lives one Saxon, will be neither peace nor law!
Now graith* my great horse, trusty squires, and do my armour
    on,
And let us see if this mote last!" And so Gwesklen was gone.

* Arm.

IV.

The Captain of Pestivien to the donjon tower he ran,
And at Lord Gwesklen japed his jape, down from the bartizan:
"Oh! is't to dance a dance you've come, you and your merry
    men,
That all so bravely harnessed ye seek Pestivien?"

"On a dancing-errand, Saxon, we *are* come, by my fay:
But 'tis *we* will pipe, and *you* shall dance, and eke the pipers
    pay.
We'll gar you dance so loath and long that you'll pray the dance
    were done;
And when we're tired of piping, there's the foul fiend shall
    pipe on!"

The first stroke that Lord Gwesklen struck, the walls to ground
    were thrown,
That the strong castle shrunk and shook to its foundation-stone.
The second stroke Lord Gwesklen struck, three towers were
    lying low,
And twice a hundred men went down, and well as many mo.

The third stroke that Lord Gwesklen struck, the gates were beaten in,
And the Bretons they were masters, walls without and courts within.

They've fired the hold, they've burnt the mould, and slockened*
it in blood;
The ploughman sings as he ploughs o'er the ground where Pestien stood:
John the Saxon, felon traitor and rank reiver though he be,
Long as the rocks of Maël shall stand shall ne'er hold Brittanie!

* Quenched.

THE WEDDING-GIRDLE.

(SEIZEN EURED.)

[The Breton expedition into Wales to which this ballad refers was undertaken under Jean de Rieuk, or De Rieux, Marshal of Brittany (in 1405), in aid of Owen Glendwr's rising against the English rule.]

I.

HAD not been betrothed but a night and eke a day,
When at the orders of my Lord de Rieux I must away;
Must march with that bold Baron, in aid, if aid may be,
Of the good Prince Owen Glendwr and the Bretons over sea.

"Now busk and boune, my little foot-page, and run beside my rein:
To say farewell to my betrothed my heart within is fain:

I must bid my betrothed farewell, the ladye I love best,
Or well I wot my heart for grief will break within my breast."

As he rode to her castle-wall he shook like an aspen tree ;
As he rode through her castle-gate his heart beat heavily.
"Now enter in, my gentle Lord, and draw the fire anigh,
That I may spread the board anon, and feast thee daintily."

"Saving your grace, good aunt, for me let never board be dight;
I come but to bid her farewell that yestreen gave me her plight."
When the good dame this heard the shoes from off her feet she laid,
And gat her in her stocking-feet upon her daughter's bed.

On the bed-stock she hath mounted, and hath bent her o'er the bed :
"Awake, awake, my Loïda, lift up thy pretty head,
And busk thee, busk thee, my bonny bairn, and lay thy night-rail by,
And speak a word to thy true love, who hath come to bid good-bye."

Then up from between the sheets sprang the maiden all a-glow,
And jet-black was the hair that fell on her shoulders white as
    snow.
" Alack and woe, my leman sweet, my Loïda, woe is me,
The time is come I must aboard and sail away from thee

" To Saxon-land, to follow the banner of my Lord,
And God he knows the heavy grief that in my heart I board."
" Now, in God's name, my own true love, sail not away from
    me :
The wind is ever changeful, and traitor is the sea.

" If 'twere thine evil hap to die, think of my heavy pain :
With hungering for news of thee my heart will break in twain.
From fisher's hut to fisher's hut I'll pace the salt sea strand :
What word, what word of him that hath my troth and heart
    and hand ?"

Oh ! sore she cried, and sore he tried to cheer her in her woe :
" Now dry thine eyes, my Loïda, and weep not for me so :
A girdle I will bring thee from o'er sea—a girdle fair—
A wedding-girdle of the blue, set all with rubies rare."

'Twas a sight to see that woeful knight as he sat by the ingle-
    glow,
His ladye-love upon his knee, her pretty head bent low,
Her two arms twined about his neck—both silent, but for
    weeping;
Till the morn should rise to part them their last sad love-tryst
    keeping.

With the first light of the morning that heavy knight 'gan
    say:
"The red cock crows, my darling, to tell the break of day."
"Now nay, now nay, my own true love; trust me, 'tis night-
    time still:
'Tis but the moon that shineth, that shineth on the hill."

"Now nay, now nay, it is the sun through the door-chinks
    comes a-glow;
'Tis time that I should leave thee, across the sea to go."
He's gone, and aye as thence he went the daws they chattered
    free:
"An' if the sea be traitor, worse traitors women be."

II.

On Saint John's Day, in the autumn, that maid was heard to say:
"I saw, far out upon the waves, from the mountains of Aré,
I saw far out a gallant ship, sore beaten by the sea,
And high upon the after-deck he stood that loveth me.

"All in his hand he held a sword, and a sore fight there was set,
And the dead lay thick about him, and his shirt with blood was wet:
My love and life are twinned,* alack!" She made no more ado,
But when the new-year's day came round, she had plighted troth anew.

But ere long there came tidings, tidings of happy strain:
The war, the war is over—the good knight is come again;
Has come again to his manor, in gladsomeness and glee,
This night he's boune to his ladye-love, his own betrothed to see.

As he came near the castle he heard the rotes sound clear,
And saw i' the castle windows the lights shine far and near:

* Separated.

"Say, merry new-year's bedesmen,* that by tower and town go
   free,
What mirth is in yon castle?—what means this minstrelsy?"

"They are the merry rote-players, a playing two and two,
'Now room for the milk-potage† that the door-stead passes
   through.'
They are the merry rote-players, a playing three and three,
'Now room for the milk-potage in the house that enters free.'"

III.

The beggars‡ bid to the wedding to their supper were addrest,
When in came an errant beggar-man, was not a bidden guest:
"Now largesse, of your courtesy, largesse of board and bed,
The night is come, I have no home, nor place to lay my head."

---

* *Eginanerien*, the beggars who at Christmas-time traverse the country asking a new-year's alms, with the cry "Eghinad d'é" ("a new-year's gift for me"), popularly contracted into *Eghina'ñi*, to a corruption of which some etymologists refer the "Hogmanay," the new-year's cry in Scotland.

† The popular wedding-air in Brittany. The milk-potage is the special dish of the new-married pair at the wedding-supper.

‡ Beggars in Brittany are among the most honoured guests at weddings, funerals, saints'-days, and all social gatherings with anything of solemnity about them.

"Now Heaven forefend, poor beggar, but thou should'st find a
    bed ;
And for thee as for the others the supper-board is spread :
Draw nigh, good man, and enter the manor, in God's name ;
My lord and I that serve the rest, we will serve thee the
    same."

The first dance that they danced in hall, the ladye spoke him
    fair :
"What aileth thee, poor beggar-man, that so still thou sittest
    there ?"
"There's nothing ails me, ladye : no cause have I therefore,
But that the way was weary, and my limbs are stiff and
    sore."

The second dance they danced in hall, outspake the bride once
    more :
"Art thou still weary, my good man, that thou tak'st not the
    floor ?"
"Oh, yes ! I am too weary for dancing, ladye fair :
And 'tis not alone I am weary, but a weight at my heart I
    bear."

The third dance that they danced in hall, the bride smiled fair
    and free,
And she came unto the beggar-man and said: "Come, dance
    with me!"
"It is an honour ill befits to the like o' me to pay;
But as 'tis offered, it were the part of a churl to say thee
    nay."

And as they moved along the dance, he stooped for her to
    hear;
And oh! but I ween the lips were green that whispered in her
    ear:
"What hast thou done with the red-gold ring ye had of me,
    fair May,
On the threshold of this chamber, was a year ago to-day?"

'Twas uplift eyes and hard-wrung hands, as grievously she
    cried:
"Till now I lived without a grief, and so hoped to have died:
I thought I was a widow, now I have husbands twain."
"'Twas ill-thought, my fair ladye, for husband thou hast
    nane."

He hath drawn a dagger beneath his coat that hung beside his
    knee,
And he hath stricken a stroke at her that garred the blood to
    flee;
That down she fell on her bended knees, and her head she hung
    aside:
"My God! my God!" was all she said—and with the word she
    died.

IV.

In Daoulaz Abbey-church stands Our Ladye carven fair,
That a girdle set with rubies from over sea doth wear:
Who gave that ruby girdle to Our Ladye if you'd weet,
Ask of the monk that lieth a penitent at her feet.

PART II.

SONGS USED ON DOMESTIC AND FESTIVE OCCASIONS.

THE FLOWERS OF MAY.

(BLEUNIOU MAE.)

[IN the districts of Cornouaille and about Vannes they have a pretty funeral fashion, of covering with flowers the biers of young girls who die in the month of May.* Such deaths are regarded as ominous of happiness hereafter, and sick girls pray to be spared till the flowers of May come back, if death seem to be darkening over them before the month; or to be taken before the flowers of May are withered, if life and flowers are waning together. The following song on this touching theme is much sung in Cornouaille, and is ascribed to two peasant sisters, still living, the authoresses of a charming little song called "The Swallows," which will be found in this volume. The delicacy, tenderness, and piety of this pathetic idyll are characteristic of the Breton; and these qualities are found among the peasantry of Brittany —rude and stern almost to gloom as they are—more than among any other class of the country.]

I.

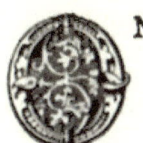

N the sea-shore who Jeff had seen
With rosy cheeks and eyes of sheen;

Who for the pardon had seen her start,
Had felt the happier in his heart:

---

* The same usage is preserved in South Wales. M. de la Villemarqué remarks on the tender use Shakspeare has made of it in "Cymbeline," in the speech he puts into the mouth of Arviragus over the body of Imogene.

But he that had seen her on her bed,
Had tears of pity for her shed,

To see the sweet sick maiden laid,
Pale as a lily in summer-shade.

To her companions she said,
That sat beside her on her bed :

" My friends, if loving friends ye be,
In God's name, do not weep for me.

" You know all living death must dree ;
God's own self died—died on the tree."

II.

As I went for water to the spring
I heard the nightingale sweetly sing :

" The month of May is passing e'en now,
And with it the blossom on the bough.

"The happiest lot from life they bring,
The young whom death takes in the spring.

"Ev'n as the rose drops from the spray,
So youth from life doth fall away.

"Those who die ere this week is flown,
All with fresh flowers shall be strown;

"And from those flowers shall soar heaven-high,
As from the rose-cup the butterfly."

III.

"Jeffik! Jeffik! did you not hear
The nightingale's song so sweet and clear?

"'The month of May is passing e'en now,
And with it the blossom on the bough.'"

When this she heard, the gentle maid,
Crosswise her two pale hands she laid:

"I will say an *Ave Marie*,
Our Ladye sweet, in honour of thee:

"That it may please our God, thy Son,
To look with pity me upon;

"That grace to pass quick me be given,
And wait for those I love in Heaven."

The *Ave Marie* was hardly said,
When gently sank her gentle head:

The pale head sank, no more to rise;
The eyelids closed upon the eyes.

Just then beyond the court-yard pale
Was heard to sing the nightingale:

"The happiest lot from life they bring,
The young whom death takes in the spring.

"Happy the young whose biers are strown
With spring-flowers, fair and freshly blown."

THE ASKING OF THE BRIDE.

(AR GOULENN.)

[MARRIAGE in Brittany is preceded by a whole series of regulated ceremonials, to which, in the district of Cornouaille especially, it is matter of religion to adhere with the utmost scrupulousness. When a young man thinks himself in a position to marry, his first recourse is to the tailor, the recognised marriage-broker of every Breton village. He it is who is supposed to know all the eligible *partis* of both sexes—their means, tastes, the wealth of their parents, the marriage portions, and "plenishing" they can respectively bring with them. When the tailor has received his commission to open negotiations with the selected maiden, he visits her parents' farm, accosts her, generally alone, and puts forward in their best light the means, looks, and accomplishments of his client. If these find favour in the girl's sight, he is referred by her to the parents. If they approve the match, the tailor formally assumes the functions of Basvalan,[*] or "messenger of marriage," and, wearing one red and one violet stocking, brings the wooer, accompanied by his nearest male relative, to the home of his intended.

This step is called the "asking of conference." The heads of the two families make acquaintance, while the lovers are left to converse apart. When they have wooed and whispered their fill, they join their parents hand in hand, wine and white bread are brought out, the young pair drink from the same glass and eat with the same knife, the bases of the marriage treaty are fixed, and a day is settled for the meeting of the two families.

This is called the *velladen*, or view, and takes place at the house of the girl.

---

[*] From *baz*, a rod, and *valan*, the broom, in allusion to the twig of flowering broom which he carries as his wand of office.

Everything is done by her parents, by display of their own havings—in furniture, linen, money, plate, provisions, stock, live and dead, implements, &c. &c.—or by borrowing from neighbours, to make the most imposing show of wealth. At this meeting of the families the conditions of the contract are finally settled.

A week before the marriage, the young couple—he accompanied by the principal bridesmaid, she by the "best-man," bearing white wands—go round the neighbourhood to deliver their invitations to the wedding, which is formally done in verses setting out time and place, and interspersed with prayers and signs of the cross.

At last comes the wedding-day. And now the functions of the *Baswalan* and the *Brwtaŷr*, or "defender," who represents the reluctance of the bride, as the *Baswalan* the passions of the bridegroom, assume their full importance in the symbolical scene which is transacted in the verses which follow, or in others of the same character, for both *Baswalan* and *Brwtaŷr* may be their own poets, so that they adhere to the regulated course of the allegory.]

THE MESSENGER OF MARRIAGE.

IN the name of Father, Son,
And Holy Ghost, God, three in one,
Blessing rest on this roof-tree,
And more joy than I bring with me.

THE DEFENDER.

What has happ'd, good friend, I pray,
To drive the joy from thy heart away?

THE MESSENGER.

In my cote, my pigeon's love,
I had a pretty little dove,

When the spar-hawk, like a flame,
Or a wind, down swooping came;
My little dove he scared away,
Where she's flown to none can say.

THE DEFENDER.

Thou look'st mighty smart and trim
For one whose eyes in sorrow swim:
Thy yellow hair thou hast combed out,
As if bound for a dancing-bout.

THE MESSENGER.

Now cease, good friend, thy jesting keen;
My little white dove say hast thou seen?
Merry man shall I never be
Till again my pretty dove I see.

THE DEFENDER.

Of thy pigeon no news I know,
Nor yet of thy dove as white as snow.

THE MESSENGER.

'Tis false, young man, the word you say;
The neighbours saw it fly this way:

Over your court they saw it fly,
And light in the orchard-plot hard by.

THE DEFENDER.

Of thy little dove as white as snow,
Nor yet of thy pigeon, no news I know.

THE MESSENGER.

My pigeon he will waste away,
If his sweet mate long from him stay;
My hapless pigeon he will die—
Through the key-hole I must spy.

THE DEFENDER.

Hold there, friend; thou shalt not go
I'll look myself and let thee know.

[*He goes into the house, and returns immediately.*
In our courtyard I have been,
Ne'er a dove there have I seen;
But I found great wealth of posies,
Bloom of lilacs, flush of roses:
Chief, a dainty little rose
That at the hedge corner grows.

I will fetch it, an you will,
Heart and eyes with joy to fill.
> *[He goes into the house again, and
> returns leading a little girl.*

THE MESSENGER.

Pretty flowret, fair thou art,
Fit to gladden a man's heart:
Were my pigeon a drop of dew,
He would sink thy breast into.
> *[After a pause.*

To the loft I'll climb anon,
Thither she perchance has flown.

THE DEFENDER.

Hold thee, friend, thou shalt not go:
I'll look myself and let thee know.
> *[He goes into the house, and returns
> with the good-wife.*

In the loft I've sought all round,
But thy dove I have not found;
Only I have found an ear
Left from harvest—it is here:

Stick it in thy hat, if so
Consolation thou mayst know.

THE MESSENGER.

Not more grains are in the ear
Than my dove shall nestlings bear,
Under snowy wings and breast,
Brooding gently, in the nest.
[After a pause
To the field in search I'll go.

THE DEFENDER.

Nay, good friend, thou shalt not so.
Wherefore soil thy dainty shoon?
I will bring thee tidings soon.
*[He enters the house, and returns
with the grandmother.*
Of your dove I saw no trace,
Nothing found I in the place
But this apple, wrinkled, old,
Hid in leaves, and left on mould:
Put it in your pocket, straight,
Give your pigeon it to eat,
And he'll cease to mourn his mate.

THE ASKING OF THE BRIDE.

THE MESSENGER.

Thanks, good friend; sound fruit is sound,
Though 'tis wrinkled round and round;
Savour sweet with age is found.
But for your apple nought I care,
Nor for your flower, nor for your ear,
All on my dove is set my mind:
I'll go myself my dove to find!

THE DEFENDER.

Foregad, but thou'rt an artful hand:
Come in with me, nor longer stand.
Thy little dove, she is not lost,
I've kept her with much care and cost;
All in a cage of ivorie,
Of silver and gold its bars they be.
There she sits, both glad and gay,
Dainty and decked in her best array!

> [*The Messenger is admitted into the house. He takes his seat for a moment at table, then retires to introduce the future bridegroom. As soon as he appears the bride's father presents him with a horse-girth, which he passes round the bride's waist; while he is buckling and unbuckling it, the Defender sings as follows:* —

THE GIRTH.

(AR GOURIZ.)

Prancing free in the meadows green,
An unbroke filly I have seen:

Nothing she recked but to prance and play
Through the meadow the live-long day;

Upon the sweet spring-grass to feed,
And drink of the streamlet in the mead.

Sudden along the way did fare,
A bachelor so debonair,

So young, so shapely, of step so light,
His clothes with gold and silver bright,

That the filly stood all at gaze,
And for the sight forgot to graze.

Then slow and softly near she drew,
And reached her neck his hand unto:

With gentle hand he hath stroked her skin,
And laid to her muzzle, cheek and chin;

And then he hath kissed her fair and free,
And oh, but a happy filly was she!

Then in her mouth a bit he hath placed,
And round her body a girth hath laced.

Then lightly on her back he hath leapt,
And away with him the filly stept!

This song sung, the bride-elect kneels at the feet of the oldest member of the family, while the poet of the occasion—often a wandering man, at once bard and beggar, but always treated with respect—invokes on her head all blessings of God, the Virgin, the Saints, and the departed of her own blood for generations back. The "best-woman" then raises her up, and the "defender" puts her hand in that of her betrothed, makes them exchange rings and swear to be as true to each other in this world as ring is to finger, that they may be eternally united in the next. He then recites aloud the *Paternoster*, the *Ave*, and the *De Profundis*. Soon after the bride-elect, who has retired, appears again, led by the "best-man," with as many rows of silver lace on her sleeve as she brings thousands of francs for her portion. The bridegroom-elect follows with the "best-woman;" the relations come after. The "messenger of marriage" brings out the bridegroom's horse and holds his stirrup while he mounts; the "defender" takes the bride-elect in his arms and sets her behind her destined husband. After them all mount and ride, at racing pace and often across country, to the church. The first who reaches it wins a sheep; the second, a bunch of ribbons.

In some cantons, adds M. de la Villemarqué,—from whom, and M. de Souvestre, these details are taken,—when the rector leaves the altar for the sacristy, the wedding party accompany him. The "best-man" carries under his arm a basket covered with a napkin, in which is a loaf of white bread and a bottle of wine. This the rector, after crossing the loaf with the knife's point, cuts and divides a morsel between the newly-married pair. He then pours the wine into a silver cup, from which the husband drinks and passes the cup to his wife.

On leaving the church, amidst the firing of guns, the explosions of squibs and crackers, the shrill notes of the *biniou*,* and the thump and jingle of the tambourine, the procession is reformed for the bride's house, where the feast is spread.

---

* A rude kind of oboe.

The rooms are hung with white sheets, and decorated with nosegays and garlands. Tables are spread wherever they will stand, often overflowing the house into the courtyard. At the end of one of them sits the bride, under an arch of flowers and foliage. As the guests take their seats an old man recites the *Benedicite*. Each course is ushered in with a burst of music, and followed by a dance; and the whole night is often spent at table.

The day after the marriage is "the day of the poor." The beggars and tramps assemble by hundreds: they consume the remains of the marriage feast, the bride herself waiting on the women, the bridegroom on the men. Before the second course the bride and bridegroom lead off the dance with the most venerable of the beggars, male and female; while songs are sung in honour of the liberality of the young couple, in which are lavished prayers for long life, prosperity, and fair issue.

The beggars leave the house invoking the blessing of Heaven on it and its owners.

There is something strangely impressive to us who are taught to regard poverty almost as a crime, and to hold beggars as the very scum of the community, in the respect, almost reverence, with which these penniless and houseless outcasts are regarded in Brittany. Something of the same kind may be seen in Ireland. This courteous pity for poverty seems due, in part at least, to Celtic feelings and usages, though the teaching of the Roman Catholic Church may have a good deal to do with it.

THE SONG OF THE JUNE FEAST.

(AR MIZ EVEN.)

[This is one of the most ancient Breton festivals—evidently a relic of the Druidic ceremonies of the summer solstice. It is now rare, being confined, says M. de la Villemarqué, to some cantons of Vannes and a few villages of Cornouaille.

The villagers of both sexes gather at some dolmen, or Druid stone, every Saturday of June at four in the afternoon. Each year's festival has a "Master" (*parron*, patron) selected among the handsomest and most agile of the youth, who chooses a maiden as queen of the day by placing on her finger a silver ring. His badge of office is a knot of ribbons, blue, green, and white, which at the end of the festival he transmits, with his dignity, by fastening it to the button-hole of the successor whom he is empowered to appoint.

The song which follows is the consecrated dialogue between the last year's master and mistress, and the address of the new master to the mistress of his choice.]

THE PAST MASTER (*to the past mistress*).

GOOD day to you, sweet gossip; greeting and fair good day:
It is an honest love and true that brings me all this way.

THE PAST MISTRESS.

Nay, never fancy, bachelor, I your betrothed must be,
All for a ring of silver that you have given to me.
Take back your ring of silver, and give or keep it still;
Of love for it, or love for you, I feel no want nor will.
There was a time, but it is past for me this many a day,
When for a smile, and but a smile, I gave my heart away:
But time has made me wiser, and hath flouted me full sore;
Let smile who will, and ne'er so sweet, but I will laugh no more.

THE PAST MASTER.

When I was young, three ribbons at my button I did show;
One was green, and one was blue, and the third was white as snow.
That green ribbon in honour of my gossip fair I wore,
For true and tender was the love in my heart for her I bore.
The white ribbon I wore in the eye of day to show,
A token of the spotless love that was betwixt us two.
The blue ribbon I wore to mark that at peace with her I'd be:
And ever as I look at it my sighs fall heavilie.
I'm left alone, now she is flown, alack and well-a-day!
As the wanton little pigeon from the old cote flies away.

THE NEW MASTER (*to his mistress*).

The summer is new comen in, with the pleasant month of June,
When youths and maids walk hand in hand, with happy hearts
    in tune:
The flowers they are open in the meadow-lands to-day,
And young folks' hearts are open too, where'er they go or stay.
See the white bloom on the hawthorn, how purely sweet it
    smells;
See how little birds are pairing in the dingles and the dells.
Then come away, my sweetheart, come walk the woods with me,
We will hear the wind a-rustle in the branches of the tree;
And the water of the streamlet the pebbles murmuring o'er,
And the birds in the tall tree-tops that their merry music pour:
Each making its own melody according to its kind,
A music that will make for us glad heart and quiet mind.

THE SONG OF THE NEW THRESHING-FLOOR.

(SON LEUR-NEVEZ.)

[The inauguration of a new threshing-floor in Brittany is a great "frolic." When the old floor has grown rough and unfit for service, the farmer announces a new threshing-floor. His neighbours assemble over-night with their carts laden with clay and water-barrels, taking up the best points for a gallop to the spot, when the first-arrived wins a knot of ribbon. The clay is rapidly unloaded, the water poured over it; the horses, with be-ribboned manes and tails, are driven round and round to work the puddle into consistence: sometimes a table is spread in the centre of the new floor, a chair set on it, and the prettiest girl of the place kept a prisoner in it till she is set free on payment of some merry forfeit. A week after, when the clay has hardened sufficiently, the new floor becomes a ball-room, and long chains of dancers, or rounds of young girls, carrying on their heads full milk-pails or crocks filled with flowers, whirl merrily about it to the music of a rote or bagpipe. The favourite figures are those interminable interlacings which may still be seen in some of our Cornish festivals—notably on Furry-Day at Helston, or at Penzance on the Eves of St. John and St. Peter. The dance is often followed by wrestling-matches—always a Celtic sport, and only practised, among ourselves, on the Celtic side of the island.]

O ope a new threshing-floor all were gone,
And of the party I was one;

To open a floor with dance and play,
I was not one at home to stay.

Of young lads there was plenty there,
And plenty, I ween, of lasses fair.

Oh, but my heart did jig away,
Soon as I heard the music play!

I saw a maid in the measure move,
She was shy as a turtle-dove:

Bright her eyes as the drops that run
On a branch of may in the rising sun;

Blue her eyes as the flax full blown,
White her teeth as the whitest stone;

A laugh on her lip and a light in her ee,
And oh, but she gave a look at me.

I looked, but for manners awhile did stand,
Before I made bold to ask her hand;

To ask her hand for a jabadaou,*
And soon we were leading the measure true.

* The favourite dance of Cornouaille.

And we danced and danced, till by degrees,
Her wee white hand I ventured to squeeze;

And then she smiled, oh, she smiled on me—
Not an angel of Heaven could sweeter be:

And I smiled back her smile again,
And since but for her my heart is fain.

I will go to see her to-night,
With a velvet band and a cross so bright;

A band of black velvet and cross so rare,
My fairing from St. Nicholas' fair:

St. Nicholas,* our patron true—
On her small white neck how brave 'twill shew.

And I'll take thee a ring of the silver fine,
For that pretty slender finger o' thine;

On her small finger a keepsake to be,
That she may sometimes think of me.

* The fête of St. Nicholas is emphatically the lover's festival in Brittany, and keepsakes and fairings bought on that day have a special virtue.

THE SONG OF THE NEW THRESHING-FLOOR.

As I came back from seeing my sweet,
I met the old tailor in the street;

I met the old tailor coming along,—
And he it was that made this song.

THE SHEPHERD'S CALL.

(ANN ALIKÊ.)

[CHILDHOOD has its special festival in Brittany. It is celebrated at the close of autumn, and is called "The Shepherd's Holiday." The scene is generally some wide heath, whither the young shepherds and shepherdesses are accustomed to drive their flocks for pasture. Hither parents bring their boys and girls, between nine and twelve years old, with good store of butter, milk, fruit, and cakes. After a merry pic-nic, some reverend senior of the party sings to the children a series of moral precepts—called *Kentel ar Vugale* (the children's lesson): then follows the indispensable dance, and as they wind their way homewards they sing this old song. Its Breton name is derived from the call which the little shepherds, boy and girl, shout to each other from hill-side to hill-side. The boy begins, "Ali, kê! ali, kê! ali, kê!" ("a warning, come!")

Then, naming the girl he wishes to call, he adds—

Lê ("hear").

If she be indisposed for a rejoinder, she calls—

Néann-ked-dê ("I won't come").

If she be socially disposed, her answer is—

Mé ia! ia ("I come; yes").

Then the boy strikes up this song, to the last stanza, which the girl sings, with variations.]

THE SHEPHERD'S CALL.

AS I rose on Sunday morning to drive the kine to lea,
    I heard my sweetheart singing—by the voice I knew 'twas she;
I heard my sweetheart singing, singing gay on the hill-side,
And I made a song to sing with her, across the valley wide.

The first time I set eyes on Mac'haidik, my sweet May,
Was at her first communion upon an Easter-day,
In the parish-church of Foësnant, 'mong her mates in age and size:
She was twelve years old,—my darling,—and I was twelve likewise.

Like golden blossom of the broom, or wild-rose sweet and small,
Like wild-rose in a heath-brake, shone my fair among them all:
All the time the mass was serving I had only eyes for her,
And the more I gazed upon her, the more love my heart did stir.

I've a full-fruited apple-tree in my mother's orchard-ground,
It has green turf about it, and an arbour built around:

When my sweet May, my best belov'd, deigns come to visit me,
We will sit, I and my sweet, in the shadow of that tree;

I'll pull for her the apple that has the rosiest skin,
Tie her a posy, with my flower, a marigold, therein—
A marigold all withered, as for-pined my cheek you see,
For not one tender kiss of love have I yet had from thee.

She answers.

Now hold thy peace, my sweetheart, and soon; and sing no
    mo:
Folk will hear you through the valley, as their way to mass
    they go.
Another time when on the heath we meet, and there's none to
    see,
One little tender love-kiss I will give you,—or two, maybe.

THE LEPER.

(AR C'HAKOUZ.)

[The leprosy appeared in Brittany near the end of the twelfth century. The unhappy creatures attacked by it were cut off from fellowship with their kind, confined to certain towns and certain quarters of those towns, had their own leper priests, leper churches, leper graves. In later times, the leper was allowed to dwell outside the gates of walled cities, and to carry on the business of rope-making; but he was still cut off from the dwellings, worship, society, and joys of those around him.

There was something horribly significant in the ceremonial which severed the leper from his fellow-creatures.

When the disease showed itself, a solemn procession, the priest at its head, visited the house: the priest exhorted the leper to resignation, stripped him of his clothes, giving him a black hooded cloak in exchange, sprinkled him with holy water, and conducted him to the church, where he listened to the death-mass kneeling, with corpse candles about him, and covered with a pall, as if he had been dead. He was then sprinkled afresh with holy water, the *Libera nos Domine* was sung, and he was led to the dwelling set apart for him, which was furnished with a bed, a press, a table, a chair, an earthen pot, and a lamp. There were given to him a hood and robe, with a red cross on the shoulder, a coverlet, a barrel, a funnel, a pair of clappers (to warn people from his way), a leathern girdle, and a birchen staff.

On the threshold the priest exhorted him once more to resignation, warned him never to go out of his hut without his black hood and his red cross: to enter neither into church, house, nor tavern, mill nor bake-house: not to wash, body or clothes, in spring or running stream: not to show himself at holiday, pardon, or public assembly: never to touch wares in market except with his staff and without speaking: never to answer with the wind, to walk at night in hollow ways, or to caress children or give them anything. Then he flung a handful of earth on his feet, and left him alone, in the name of Father, Son, and Holy Ghost. If the man, thus doomed to death in life, had children, they were not baptised with others, but apart, and the water that had touched them was thrown out as polluted. When he died he was buried under the floor of his hut.

The *c'hakous*, as they were called in Brittany, became extinct in the fifteenth century; but the trades of rope-maker and cooper, formerly practised by them, are still regarded with a lingering feeling of contempt and aversion. The lepers are the subjects of many popular songs and ballads—turning naturally on the wretchedness of their lot, especially on their separation from those they love. This is the theme of the following dialogue between a leper and his love.]

HE.

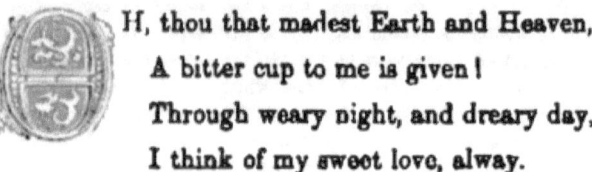H, thou that madest Earth and Heaven,
A bitter cup to me is given!
Through weary night, and dreary day,
I think of my sweet love, alway.

My mortal sickness to my bed
Holdeth close-bound my stricken head:
If my sweet love could come to me,
Ah, soon consolèd I should be.

Welcome as morning-star that shows
After a night of weary woes,
My gentle maiden's face would be,
If she could come to comfort me.

If she but touched with her sweet lip
My drinking-cup's extremest tip ;
Drinking where she had drunk before,
Straightway would vanish scab and sore.

The heart that thou didst give to me,
Oh, my beloved, to keep for thee,
I have not lost, nor squandered it,
Nor to an evil use have set.

The heart that thou didst give to me,
Oh, my beloved, to keep for thee,
I have it mingled up with mine:
Which is my heart, and which is thine?

SHE.

Who is it talketh to me so,
That am as black as any crow?

HE.

If you were black as mulberriè,
For him that loves you, white you'd be.

SHE.

Young man, it is not sooth you say :
To you I gave no heart away :
My maiden-love I gave you not :
You are a leper, well I wot.

HE.

Like to an apple on the bough
Is woman's heart, I do avow :
Fair is the apple's hue and form,
But in its heart it hides a worm.

Like to the leaf upon the spray
Is beauty in a maiden-May :
The leaf it droppeth to the ground,
So lovely looks to fade are found.

Like the blue flower beside the stream,
The love of a young girl I deem :
The little flower, of sunlight fain,
Will sometime turn and turn again.

The little flower it turns o' days,
The young girl's love it turns always ;
The flower is by the stream swept down,
Forgettings traitor-memories drown.

I am a youthful clerk, and poor,
I am the son of Iann Kaour ;
Three years of study I was fain,
Now I shall ne'er to school again.

But soon, after brief space of woe,
From my own folk I hence shall go :
Soon death will come, to my desire,
And purgatory's cleansing fire.

THE MILLER'S WIFE OF PONTARO.

(MELINEREZ PONTARO.)

AT Bannalek is a pardon gay
    Where pretty girls are stol'n away;—
      And my mill-wheels cry
        Diga-diga-di ;
      And my mill-wheels say
        Diga-diga-da !

Thither come gallants so fine and fair,
Great horses with trappings rich and rare,

And white-plumed beavers on waving curls,
To win the fancies of pretty girls.

Humpy Guillaouik* is wroth and wae,
His pretty Fantik is won away.

    * The Breton equivalent for Willikin.

"Little snip, look not so crazed and crost,
Your pretty Fantik is not lost:

"Safe at Pontaro mill is she,
In the young Baron's companie."

"Toc! toc! toc! Miller—out and alack!
Give me my pretty Fantik back."

"I ne'er saw your Fanchon, Humpy Will,
Ne'er save once, at the Baron's mill;

"Once, by the bridge, all in her best,
With a little rose upon her breast;

"Her coif was whiter than new-fallen snow,
It ne'er was gift of yours, I know;

"And her black velvet bodice was jimp and tight,
Laced with a lace of silver-white.

"A basket she bore on her arm so fair,
Filled with fruits gold-ripe and rare;

" Fruits in the manor-garden grown,
And flowers, poor snip, above them strown.

" She looked at her face in the water clear—
I trow 'twas no face to flout or fleer:

" And aye she sung—'tis true, o' my life—
' Well is it with the miller's wife:

" ' To be a miller's wife 's my will—
The miller's, at the young Baron's mill.' "

" Miller, thy japes and jeers restrain,
Give me my pretty Fantik again."

" Though you count me five hundred crowns
Your Fantik shall be no such clown's:

" Your Fanchon ne'er shall be at your will,
Here she shall bide, in the Baron's mill:

" Your Fantik home you shall never bring,—
Upon her finger I've put my ring.

"In Lord Ewen's mill she shall abide—
There's a man for a woman's pride!"

The men of the mill, they were merry men,
They stinted not singing—but nor ben—

Singing so loud and whistling so clear—
"Pancakes and butter is dainty fare;

"Pancakes well-buttered, face and back,
And a gowpen* o' meal out of every man's sack;

"A gowpen o' meal out of every man's poke,
And pretty girls, too, that can take a joke!"
   And my mill-wheels cry
    Diga-diga-di;
   And my mill-wheels say
    Diga-diga-da!

 * Handful—*Scottish.*

THE SILVER MIRRORS.

(MELLEZOUROU ARC'HANT.)

[THE Breton bride wears her coif decorated with little silver mirrors.]

LYTHE and listen, old and young,
Lythe and list to a new song

On Marchaid of Kerglujar,
Fairest maiden, near or far.

And her mother to her said,
"None so fair as my Marchaid."

"Little boots it to be fair,
Since no wooer you'll let near.

"When the apple's red and full,
Needs you lose no time to pull :

"It will fall and waste its prime,
If it be not pulled in time."

"Little one, be comforted,
In a year you shall be wed."

"And if before the year I die,
Sorely you will grieve and cry.

"If dead ere the year I be,
In a new grave bury me:

"On my grave-stead put three posies,
Two of laurel, one of roses.

"When the young clerks seek the ground,
They will deal the posies round:

"To each other they will say,
'Maiden-corpse lies here in clay;

"'Dead for longing once to wear
The silver mirrors in her hair—

"'Wayside tomb* for me were well,
Out of sound of passing bell:

"'Bell for me will never ring,
Priest o'er me will never sing.'"

* A threat of suicide.

THE CROSS BY THE WAY.

(KROAZ ANN HENT.)

SWEET in the green-wood a birdie sings,
    Golden-yellow its two bright wings,
    Red its heartikin, blue its crest:
    Oh, but it sings with the sweetest breast!

Early, early it lighted down
On the edge of my ingle-stone,
As I prayed my morning prayer,—
"Tell me thy errand, birdie fair."

Then sung it as many sweet things to me
As there are roses on the rose-tree:
"Take a sweetheart, lad, 'an you may,
To gladden your heart both night and day."

                                            D D

Past the cross by the way as I went,
Monday, I saw her, fair as a saint:
Sunday, I will go to mass,
There on the green I'll see her pass.

Water poured in a beaker clear,
Dimmer shows than the eyes of my dear;
Pearls themselves are not more bright
Than her little teeth, pure and white.

Then her hands and her cheek of snow,
Whiter than milk in a black pail, show.
Yes, if you could my sweetheart see,
She would charm the heart from thee.

Had I as many crowns at my beck,
As hath the Marquis of Poncalec;
Had I a gold-mine at my door,—
Wanting my sweetheart, I were poor.

If on my door-sill up should come
Golden flowers for furze and broom,

Till my court were with gold piled high,
Little I'd reck, but she were by.

Doves must have their close warm nest,
Corpses must have the tomb for rest;
Souls to Paradise must depart,—
And I, my love, must to thy heart.

Every Monday at dawn of day
I'll on my knees to the cross by the way;
At the new cross by the way I'll bend,
In thy honour, my gentle friend!

THE SWALLOWS.*

(AR GWENNILIED.)

To our village a pathway small
   Leadeth from the manor-hall;

A pathway whiter than 'tis wide,
And a May-bush grows beside:

Sweet thereon the May-flowers smell—
Our lord's young son, he loves them well.

I'd be a May-flower, 'an I might,
For him to cull with his hand so white;

To cull with that small hand of his,
That whiter than the May-flower is.

* Composed by the same sisters who wrote "The Flowers of May."

I would a May-flower I might be,
That on his heart he might set me.

Still from the hall away he goes
When winter crowns the house with snows;

Goes to the country of the Gaul,*
As doth the swallow, at winter-fall.

When the young year wakes germ and grain,
With the young year he comes again;

When the blue corn-flower's in the wheat,
And barley-ears wave green and sweet;

When sings the lark above the lea,
And finch and linnet on the tree;—

Comes back to us a welcome guest,
At holiday and patrons' feast.

* "Bro-chall," France, as usual in the Breton.

Oh, would that every month were May,
And every hour a holiday:

Would I could see about the sky
All the year round the swallows fly;

Could see them still, from spring to spring,
Abound our chimney on the wing!

THE POOR CLERK.*

(AR CHLOAREK PAOUR.)

MY wooden shoes I've lost them, my naked feet I've torn,
    A-following my sweeting through field and brake of thorn :
The rain may beat, and fall the sleet, and ice chill to the bone,
But they're no stay to hold away the lover from his own.

My sweeting is no older than I that love her so :
She's scarce seventeen, her face is fair, her cheeks like roses glow.
In her eyes there is a fire, sweetest speech her lips doth part ;
Her love it is a prison where I've locked up my heart.

  * An account will be found in the Introduction of the Seminarists of Tréguier, and of the circumstances under which such idylls as this are written.

F. F.

Oh, to what shall I liken her, that a wrong it shall not be?
To the pretty little white rose, that is callèd Rose-Marie?
The pearl of girls; the lily when among the flowers it grows,
The lily newly opened, among flowers about to close.

When I came to thee a-wooing, my sweet, my gentle May,
I was as is the nightingale upon the hawthorn spray:
When he would sleep the thorns they keep a pricking in his
    breast,
That he flies up perforce and sings upon the tree's tall crest.

I am as is the nightingale, or as a soul must be
That in the purgatory fires lies longing to be free,
Waiting the blessèd time when I into your house shall come,
All with the marriage-messenger,* bearing his branch of broom.

Ah, me! my stars are froward: 'gainst nature is my state;
Since in this world I came I've dreed a dark and dismal fate:
I have nor living kin nor friends, mother nor father dear,
There is no Christian on earth to wish me happy here.

      * The *basralan*. See the Songs of Marriage.

There lives no one hath had to bear so much of grief and
    shame
For your sweet sake as I have, since in this world I came;
And therefore on my bended knees, in God's dear name I sue,
Have pity on your own poor clerk, that loveth only you!

THE SONG OF THE SOULS IN PAIN.

(KANÂOUEN ANN ANAON.)

[THE "black month" (November), says M. de la Villemarqué, is the month of the dead. On All Saints' Eve (the Scotch Halloween) crowds flock to the grave-yards to pray by the family graves, to fill with holy water the little hollows left for this pious purpose in the Breton grave-stones, or, in some places, to offer libations of milk. All night masses for the dead are said, and the bells toll: in some places, after vespers the parish priest goes round in procession by torch-light to bless the tombs. In every house the cloth and the remains of the supper are left on the table, that the souls of the dead may take their seats about the board: the fire, too, is left burning on the hearth, that the dead may warm their thin hands at the embers, as they did in life. When the dead-mass has been said, the death-bell tolled, the supper eaten, and the household are a-bed, weird wailings are heard outside the door, blent with the sighing of the wind. They are the songs of the souls, who borrow the voice of the parish poor to ask the prayers of the living. This is their song.]

Y Father, Son, and Holy Ghost,
We greet this house, its head and host,
Greeting and health to great and small—
And bid you straight to praying fall.

When Death knocks with his hand so thin,
At midnight, asking to come in,

No heart but with a quake doth say,
Who is it Death would take away?

But you, be not amazed, therefor,
If we the Dead stand at the door;
'Tis Jesus bade us hither creep
To waken you, if chance you sleep.

To wake you in this house that bide,
To wake you, old and young beside,
If ruth, alack, live under sky,
For succour in God's name we cry!

Brothers and friends and kinsmen all,
In God's name hear us when we call;
In God's name pray for us, pray sore,
Our children, ah, they pray no more!

They that we fed upon the breast,
Long since to think of us have ceast:
They that we held in our heart's core,
Hold us in loving thought no more!

My son, my daughter, daintily,
On warm soft feather beds ye lie,
Whilst I your mother, I your sire,
Scorch in the purgatory fire.

All soft and still and warm you lie,
The poor souls toss in agony:
You draw your breaths in quiet sleep,
Poor souls in pain their watching keep.

A white shroud and five planks for bed,
A sack of straw beneath the head,
And over it five feet of clay,
Are all Earth's goods we take away.

We lie in fire and anguish-sweat,—
Fire over head, fire under feet,
Fire all above, fire all below—
Pray for the souls that writhe in woe!

Aforetime when on earth we moved,
Parents we had and friends that loved,

But now that we are dead and gone,
Parents and lovers we have none.

Succour, in God's name, you that may:
Unto the blessèd Virgin pray,
A drop of her dear milk to shed,
One drop, on poor souls sore bestead.

Up from your beds, and speedilìè,
And throw yourselves on bended knee,
Save those whom ailments sore make lame,
Or Death, already, calls by name!

Hearing this lamentable cry, all rise from their beds, fall on their knees, and pray God for the departed, not forgetting their representatives—the poor at the door.

The lugubrious troop passes on its way, through the bare woods, over the waste heaths, to the sound of the death-bells, and the wailing of the wind among the dead leaves, which are—says the Breton proverb—less thick on the ground in the black month, than the souls of the dead are in the air this night.

APPENDIX.

THE ORIGINAL BRETON AIRS OF SOME OF THE PRECEDING
BALLADS AND SONGS HARMONIZED.

APPENDIX.

THE Breton melodies are wild and expressive, partaking somewhat of the character of the Welsh national airs, though ruder and less complete. Some of them (as noted by M. de la Villemarqué) are so irregular, both in rhythm and diatonic progression, that it is difficult to harmonize them without alteration. Among the most unmanageable are "The Crusader's Wife," "The Falcon," and "The Nightingale," the music of which I have in consequence omitted. "Bran" and "Rohan" have no airs noted by M. de la Villemarqué. "Gwenc'hlan" and "Jaufoz" are beautifully harmonized in M. de la Villemarqué's book, and these I have adopted as they stand. I have retained the Breton words, as, owing to a peculiar deviation in the accentuation of the words as sung from that of the words as spoken (a peculiarity still retained in the modern French), it is difficult to accommodate to the airs English words, even when metrically equivalent to the Breton. This will explain some few alterations in the English words as printed in the music from the versions in the earlier part of the volume.

LAURA W. TAYLOR.

GWIN AR CHALLAOUED.
(Wine of the Gauls.)

AOTROU NANN.
(The Lord Nann.)

DIOUGAN GWENCHLAN.
(The Prediction of Gwenchlan.)

BALE ARZUR.
(The March of Arthur.)

ALAN-AL-LOUARN.
(Alan the Fox.)

226 APPENDIX.

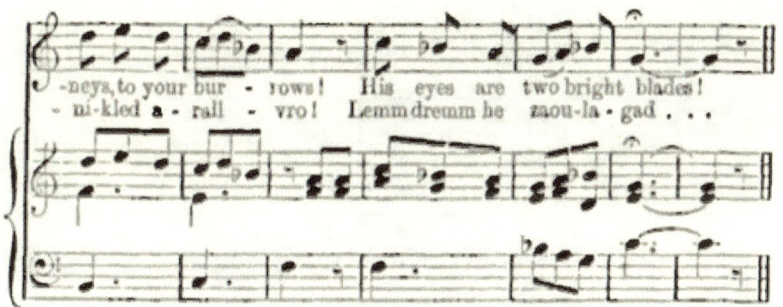

LIVADEN GERIZ.
(The Drowning of Kaer-is.)

DROUK-KINNIG NEUMENOIOU.
(THE EVIL TRIBUTE OF NOMENOE.)

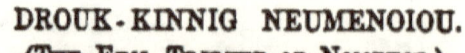

APPENDIX.

BOSEN ELLIANT.
(THE PLAGUE OF ELLIANT.)

DISTRO EUZ A VRO-ZAOZ.
(RETURN FROM SAXON LAND.)

AR BREUR MAGER.
(THE FOSTER BROTHER.)*

* It was found impossible to accommodate the rhythm and accent of the English to this air, though I have preserved the metre of the original. T. T.

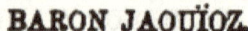

STOURM ANN TREGONT.
(The Battle of the Thirty.)

FEST AR MIZ EVEN.
(THE JUNE FEAST.)

234 APPENDIX.

ANN ALIKÉ.
(THE SHEPHERD'S CALL.)

AR C'HAKOUZ.
(The Leper.)

MELINEREZ PONTARO.

(The Miller's Wife of Pontaro.)

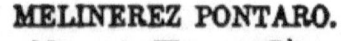

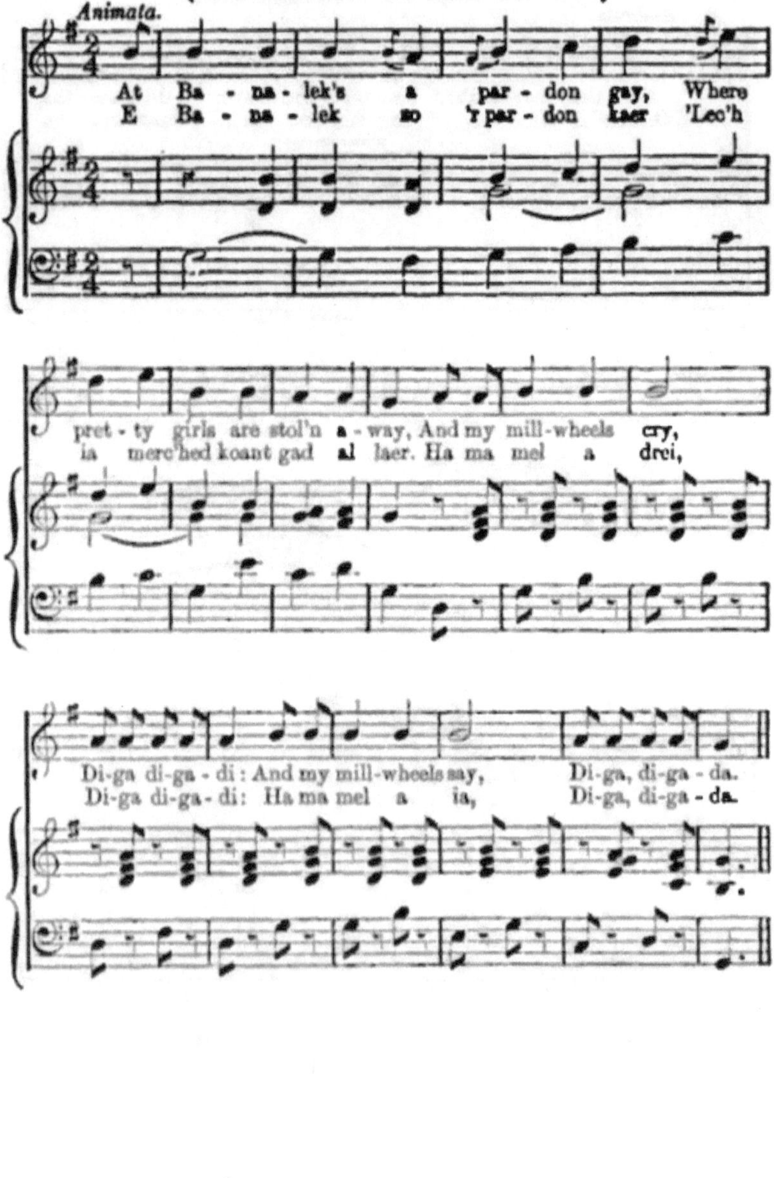

Animata.
At Ba - na - lek's a par - don gay, Where
E Ba - na - lek so 'r par - don kaer 'Leo'h
pret - ty girls are stol'n a - way, And my mill-wheels cry,
ia merc'hed koant gad al laer. Ha ma mel a drei,
Di-ga di-ga - di : And my mill-wheels say, Di-ga, di-ga - da.
Di-ga di-ga - di: Ha ma mel a ia, Di-ga, di-ga - da.

MELLEZOUROU ARC'HANT.
(The Silver Mirrors.)

KROAZ ANN HENT.
(The Cross by the Way.)

www.ingramcontent.com/pod-product-compliance
Lightning Source LLC
Chambersburg PA
CBHW021807230426
43669CB00008B/662